US NAVY SHIPS
VS
KAMIKAZES

Pacific Theater 1944–45

MARK STILLE

First published in Great Britain in 2016 by Osprey Publishing
PO Box 883, Oxford, OX1 9PL, UK
1385 Broadway, 5th Floor, New York, NY 10018, USA
E-mail: info@ospreypublishing.com

Osprey Publishing, part of Bloomsbury Publishing Plc
© 2016 Osprey Publishing Ltd.

A CIP catalogue record for this book is available from the British Library

ISBN: 978 1 4728 1273 5
PDF ISBN: 978 1 4728 1274 2
ePub ISBN: 978 1 4728 1275 9

Edited by Tony Holmes
All artwork by Jim Laurier
Index by Alan Rutter
Typeset in ITC Conduit and Adobe Garamond
Maps and formation diagrams by Boundford.com
Originated by PDQ Media, Bungay UK
Printed in China through Worldprint Ltd

16 17 18 19 20 10 9 8 7 6 5 4 3 2 1

Osprey Publishing supports the Woodland Trust, the UK's leading woodland
conservation charity. Between 2014 and 2018 our donations will be spent on
their Centenary Woods project in the UK.

www.ospreypublishing.com

USS *Laffey* (DD-724) versus kamikazes cover art

The destroyer USS *Laffey* (DD-724) has the distinction of suffering the most
concerted kamikaze attack of the entire war. Despite grievous damage, it
survived the experience and still exists today as a museum ship in Charleston,
South Carolina. On April 16, 1945, the ship's survival was very uncertain. The
destroyer was manning Radar Picket 1 and came under attack from a sizeable
proportion of the 165 suicide aircraft committed by the Japanese to *Kikusui*
No. 2. For more than two hours from 0744 hrs, the ship was targeted by at
least 23 suicide aircraft. It was hit six times and grazed twice, with three bombs
exploding on board and another two near misses being recorded. Despite this
beating, *Laffey*'s engineering plant remained operable and the destroyer was
able to maneuver in spite of rudder damage. The crew fought fires to save their
ship, which was never in danger of sinking throughout the ordeal. Considering
the scale of the attack, casualties on board were surprisingly moderate – 31
dead and 72 wounded. *Laffey* returned to the United States and was repaired,
after which it went on to serve with the fleet for a further 30 years. (Cover
artwork by Jim Laurier)

USS *Bunker Hill* (CV-17) versus kamikazes cover art

On May 11, 1945, the kamikaze came as close as they ever would to sinking an
American fleet carrier. On this day, four Zero-sens evaded radar detection and
selected USS *Bunker Hill* (CV-17) for attack, achieving complete surprise. Two
of the aircraft succeeded in striking the carrier, the first hitting aft and creating
havoc among the F4U Corsairs from VF-84 and the SB2C-3 Helldivers from
VB-84 that were parked in rows ready for their next mission. The kamikaze
pilot released his bomb prior to striking the carrier, and after penetrating parts
of the ship it exploded, causing horrendous casualties to exposed personnel.
The second Zero-sen struck the base of the island, the bomb from this aircraft
penetrating as far as the gallery deck (between the flight- and hangar decks)
prior to exploding. The bomb started a fire in the hangar among the aircraft
that were parked there. This blaze, combined with the one raging on the
flightdeck, threatened to destroy the ship. The crew fought the conflagration
from 1000 hrs until 1530 hrs, when firefighting teams finally brought the blaze
under control. The ship was saved, but it was forced out of the war. The price
paid by *Bunker Hill*'s crew was almost beyond measure – 346 killed, 43
missing, and 264 wounded. (Cover artwork by Jim Laurier)

CONTENTS

INTRODUCTION

Ever since their introduction in 1944, there has been a level of mystique associated with the kamikaze. Their background is easy to explain. The only true course for a Japanese warrior was to seek death before dishonor. Accordingly, Japanese soldiers and sailors in the opening years of the Pacific War rarely surrendered. On obscure islands, the Americans learned that their enemy would fight to the death. This included suicide to avoid surrender or, when the situation looked hopeless, a last charge to kill as many Americans as possible. These attacks were suicidal, but were only used as a last resort when all appeared hopeless. It provided the warrior with an opportunity to die in battle.

Examples abound of this phenomenon. On May 29, 1943 on Attu Island in the Aleutians, about a thousand men of the original garrison of 2,400 conducted one of the largest suicide charges of the war. Half were killed in the process of inflicting great carnage on the surprised Americans, and the other half committed suicide instead of surrendering. On Betio Island in Tarawa Atoll in the Gilbert Islands, the garrison of 3,636 Japanese went down fighting when the US Marine Corps stormed ashore in November 1943. Only 17 enemy soldiers surrendered. On Saipan Island in June 1944, less than a thousand of the original garrison of more than 31,000 soldiers and sailors were captured. The battle was capped off on July 7, 1944 when the last 3,000 defenders made a final suicidal charge.

Throughout the war there were also examples of Japanese airmen seeking death by deliberately crashing their aircraft into American ships. This was not the same as making suicide the basis for operational planning, however. This only came into effect from October 1944 when American invasion forces headed to Leyte Island, in the Philippines. Given the demonstrated ineffectiveness of conventional air attacks against the US Navy's Pacific Fleet, local Japanese command authorities opted for suicide

strikes instead. The initial success of kamikaze operations in the Philippines emboldened the Japanese to expand their use and make them the centerpiece of their operations going forward.

The largest air-sea battle of the Pacific War was fought off Okinawa in 1945. Almost 2,000 kamikazes brought death and destruction to the American fleet between April and June 1945. However, in the end, the kamikaze weapon, for all its terror and for all the carnage it caused, was ultimately ineffective as a means to turn the war in Japan's favor.

For the US Navy, the introduction of the kamikaze, which was essentially a missile using the pilot for guidance, was the ultimate threat. It had put considerable thought and immense resources into devising the means to protect its ships against air attack. By 1944 this had produced a layered defense that had provided the fleet with a high

Even before the advent of the kamikaze campaign there were many instances of Japanese pilots crashing their aircraft into American ships on an impromptu basis. The B6N2 Type 97 Carrier Attack Bomber, shown here in 1943 still carrying its torpedo, has just missed an American carrier. By late 1944 the Japanese would turn from occasional suicide attacks to a policy of mass, organized suicide attacks. (via Jim Lansdale)

The shattered wing of a kamikaze aircraft on the deck of a US Navy carrier was an all too common sight from October 1944. Despite making carriers a priority target, kamikazes were relatively ineffective against them unless the aircraft's bomb penetrated to the hangar deck and created a fire feeding on the many combustible items located there. (via Jim Lansdale)

level of protection from conventional air attack. Combined with the declining skills of Japanese aviators, the air threat to the fleet had been greatly reduced. The sudden introduction of the kamikaze in October 1944 was an unforeseen development, and it dramatically increased the air threat to the US Navy.

By the end of the Philippines campaign it was clear that the Japanese would rely on kamikazes to attack the American invasion fleets as they neared Japan. It was also clear that existing means of providing fleet air defense were insufficient. This prompted a crash program to devise methods to defeat the kamikaze threat. Amid this uncertainty, the Americans invaded Okinawa in April 1945. As expected, the Japanese responded fanatically, since Okinawa was considered part of their homeland, and because American bases on the island posed a direct threat to Japan itself. Fanatical resistance ashore by the Japanese garrison prolonged the campaign for three months. For the entirety of this period, the US Navy was forced to operate directly off the island in support of American forces ashore. This made the fleet an easy target for the kamikazes operating from bases on the southern Japanese island of Kyushu. In total, some 1,900 kamikazes were committed against the invasion fleet. These attacks caused great carnage, but failed to stop or even delay the American seizure of the island.

Following the loss of Okinawa, the last hope of the Japanese warlords was a final battle in defense of Japan in which American casualties would be so severe that some sort of negotiated peace would be possible. In these desperate days, thousands of kamikazes where prepared for action. Armageddon was avoided by the introduction of atomic weapons in August 1945 that prevented the final showdown between the kamikaze and the US Navy.

Although the space available precludes a complete treatment of all Japanese airborne suicide operations, this short book traces the story of the kamikaze's development, the American efforts to defeat it, and its impact on the war.

Groundcrew and fellow pilots wave as a Special Attack pilot taxis his bombed-up A6M5 out for takeoff from a base in the Philippines in October or November 1944. (Robert Lawson Collection, NMNA)

CHRONOLOGY

1944

October 20 First kamikaze unit readied for action.

October 25 First formal kamikaze attacks in the Philippines are launched, one escort carrier being sunk and several damaged.

November Kamikaze attacks increase against US Navy units operating near Leyte and against the Mindoro invasion force.

1945

January 4–13 American forces invade Luzon. Japanese mount heaviest kamikaze attacks to date sinking one escort carrier and sinking or damaging 46 other ships and craft.

February Kamikazes attack US Navy invasion force off Iwo Jima, sinking one escort carrier.

April 6–7 *Kikusui* No. 1 sends 335 Imperial Japanese Naval Air Force (IJNAF) and Japanese Army Air Force (JAAF) suicide aircraft against the US Navy off Okinawa.

April 12–13 *Kikusui* No. 2 sends 185 IJNAF and JAAF suicide aircraft against the US Navy off Okinawa.

April 15–16 *Kikusui* No. 3 sends 165 IJNAF and JAAF suicide aircraft against the US Navy off Okinawa.

April 27–28 *Kikusui* No. 4 sends 115 IJNAF and JAAF suicide aircraft against the US Navy off Okinawa.

May 3–4 *Kikusui* No. 5 sends 125 IJNAF and JAAF suicide aircraft against the US Navy off Okinawa.

May 10–11 *Kikusui* No. 6 sends 150 IJNAF and JAAF suicide aircraft against the US Navy off Okinawa.

May 24–25 *Kikusui* No. 7 sends 165 IJNAF and JAAF suicide aircraft against the US Navy off Okinawa.

May 27–28 *Kikusui* No. 8 sends 110 IJNAF and JAAF suicide aircraft against the US Navy off Okinawa.

June 3–7 *Kikusui* No. 9 sends 50 IJNAF and JAAF suicide aircraft against the US Navy off Okinawa.

June 21–22 *Kikusui* No. 10 sends 45 IJNAF and JAAF suicide aircraft against the US Navy off Okinawa.

July–August Japanese greatly reduce kamikaze attacks to preserve aircraft for the defense of Japan.

July 29 Destroyer USS *Callaghan* (DD-792) becomes the last US Navy ship sunk by kamikazes.

August 15 Japan surrenders, leaving thousands of kamikaze aircraft readied for action unused.

A Ki-43-II "Oscar" of the 33rd Sentai in the Philippines in late 1944. Note that the aircraft is carrying a 551lb Type 92 high explosive bomb beneath its right wing, which greatly increased its effectiveness as a kamikaze. Such a weapon was always carried in conjunction with a 200-liter drop tank beneath the opposing wing, the latter being carried both to extend the fighter's range and to offset the weight of the bomb. (via Jim Lansdale)

DESIGN AND DEVELOPMENT

THE FIRST KAMIKAZES

Although a policy of deliberately crashing aircraft into the target was not adopted until late 1944, there were documented instances before then of Japanese pilots deliberately targeting US Navy ships with their aircraft. Sometimes this was the result of a pilot deciding to do the maximum amount of damage with a damaged aircraft, and on other occasions it appeared to be deliberate from the start.

The Battle of Santa Cruz on October 26, 1942 provides an early example. The carrier USS *Hornet* (CV-8) was the target of concerted IJNAF air attack. The ship was

Proper Terminology

The term "kamikaze" was not used during the war by the Japanese. To the Japanese, the proper pronunciation of the characters that are used to describe this form of attack would be *shinbu*. However, kamikaze has become the accepted term and will be used throughout this book. The English translation for kamikaze is "divine wind". The Japanese also referred to kamikaze attacks as *tokubetsu kogeki* (special attack, abbreviated as *tokko*) and to the units conducting them as *tokubetsu kogeki tai* (or *tokko tai*).

heavily damaged, and part of the carnage was caused by a D3A Type 99 Carrier Bomber (Allied reporting name "Val") that crashed into the island and a B5N Type 97 Carrier Attack Bomber ("Kate") that struck the bow. In both instances, the aircraft were damaged during the attack and their pilots made the choice to expend themselves against the carrier. Of note, the damage caused by these aircraft was light, but the carrier was hit by two torpedoes during the attack which eventually led to its loss. Another "Kate," also damaged, flew into the destroyer USS *Smith* (DD-378) escorting the carrier USS *Enterprise* (CV-6) and created a large fire forward that killed 57 men.

The IJNAF was not the only air force crashing into ships. On May 27, 1944, a JAAF Ki-45 Type 2 Twin-engined Fighter ("Nick") hit the US Navy sub-chaser *SC-699* off Biak Island. This was another instance of the pilot making an instantaneous decision with a damaged aircraft.

Pilots and crewmen from the JAAF's Kyokko-Tai Special Attack Unit receive a farewell toast before heading off on a kamikaze mission in the Philippines in November 1944. This unit flew Type 99 Light Bombers ("Lily"). (via Edward M. Young)

ADOPTION OF THE KAMIKAZE

At the start of the war, the IJNAF's pilots were the best trained naval aviators in the world. The carrier pilots were the cream of the crop, and showed themselves to be formidable adversaries. From Pearl Harbor to the Indian Ocean and then in the carrier battles of Coral Sea and Midway, they were renowned for their prowess. Although Midway was a disaster from the standpoint that four of the IJN's fleet carriers were lost, aircrew losses were not yet crippling.

This changed during the Guadalcanal campaign, which was a grinding six-month battle of attrition. There were two carrier clashes during the campaign, and the second one in October 1942 – the Battle of Santa Cruz – was a Pyrrhic victory with Japanese aircrew losses worse than at Midway. Just as alarming, some 1,100 naval aircraft were lost during the entire campaign, along with most of their highly trained crews. This was followed by a prolonged attempt during much of 1943 to slow the American advance up through the Solomon Islands, which was composed of a constant series of aerial battles. The net effect was to gut the IJNAF's cadre of highly trained aircrew.

9

A common kamikaze aircraft was the D4Y Carrier Bomber (Allied reporting name "Judy"). Built to replace the "Val" as the standard carrier-based dive-bomber, the "Judy" was a much more capable machine with a higher top speed (up to 357mph for the most-produced variant, the D4Y3 Model 33 Suisei) and a greater payload of up to 1,764lb in a suicide role. This particular D4Y3, flown by Lt Yoshinori Yamaguchi of the 701st Kokutai, was photographed moments before it hit the deck of USS *Essex* (CV-9) on November 25, 1944. One of two kamikazes that targeted the ship, this aircraft was the only one to succeed in its mission, striking *Essex*'s flightdeck. The resulting explosion started a fire that killed 15 and injured 44. The carrier was back in action in just over two weeks, however (NARA)

The consequence of this was dramatically demonstrated in June 1944 in the largest carrier action of the war. In the Battle of the Philippine Sea, the IJN gathered a large force of nine carriers with some 430 embarked aircraft. This carefully husbanded force was committed against the American invasion of the Mariana Islands. Retention of the Marianas was considered critical since they were within Japan's inner defense zone. If these islands fell, the Americans would be in position to mount long-range air attacks from airfields against the Japanese home islands. The carrier battle did turn out to be decisive, but not in the way the Japanese had hoped. Of the nine IJN carriers brought into the battle, three were sunk, and of the 430 aircraft available before the start of the campaign, only 35 remained at the end of the battle. Most disturbingly for the IJN, the greatest massing of carrier air power in the war resulted in a total of just three US Navy ships slightly damaged and none sunk. In this battle, 60 IJNAF aircraft made bombing attacks and scored only five hits or damaging near misses. None of these caused major damage.

The Battle of the Philippine Sea resulted in the virtual annihilation of the IJN's carrier force for the remainder of the war, since there was no hope of training qualified air crew capable of taking on the US Navy's Fast Carrier Task Force.

To put it simply, conventional Japanese air attacks were increasingly ineffective. One detailed tally showed that in the first six months of 1944, 315 Japanese aircraft survived fighter interception to attack various US Navy ships. Of these, just ten percent scored a hit, which most often caused only superficial damage. Of these 315 aircraft, 106 were shot down by antiaircraft fire. Against the US Navy's Fast Carrier Task Force, from November 1943 to June 1944, the results were under five percent of aircraft hitting a target in daylight attacks and just over two percent for night attacks. In daylight, 195 aircraft made attacks and 40 percent were destroyed by antiaircraft fire.

With this backdrop, the examination of possible suicide tactics began to gain traction. Even before the debacle during the Battle of the Philippine Sea there had been discussions in 1943 among the IJN's leadership about adopting suicide tactics. By August 1944 it was widely accepted that only suicide operations could change the course of the war. The man who translated these thoughts into action was Vice Admiral Takijiro Onishi, of whom we will hear more later.

On the surface, the kamikaze was a formidable weapon, and the formal adoption of this type of suicide attack was an extraordinary opportunity to turn the course of the war. The basis for its effectiveness was its sophisticated guidance system – a human pilot with the ability to instantaneously adjust to changing situations and guide his aircraft to the target. This pilot could theoretically select the most valuable ship for attack and then fly his aircraft into its most vulnerable part. Once at the target, the pilot was trained to release his bomb to cause additional damage before his aircraft became a multi-ton projectile with the added destructive power of any unused fuel still onboard.

KAMIKAZE TACTICS

The tactics used by kamikazes from their inception in October 1944 until the end of the war changed dramatically. This was due to two factors. The biggest one was the need to train novice pilots after the initial batch of experienced volunteers was expended in the Philippines. Of course, in war, the enemy is also constantly evolving, as did the Americans to the growing threat posed by kamikaze attack. The Japanese were also forced to evolve to maintain their chances of getting the kamikazes through to their targets.

Despite the notion that crashing an aircraft into a ship was fundamentally easy, the reality is just the opposite, especially when you factor in the extensive defensive efforts made by the US Navy. Firstly, the American combat air patrol (CAP) had to be evaded. Secondly, antiaircraft fire had to be avoided. Thirdly, the pilot had to hit a fast and maneuvering target. This was difficult, even for experienced pilots. After 1944 few of the pilots on kamikaze missions were experienced, their places having been taken by new pilots with minimal training. All things considered, the rate of success achieved by kamikaze pilots was low, being something in the order of ten percent.

The tactics used in the initial attacks were primitive. Early strikes were conducted by small groups of aircraft, often numbering as few as five machines including the

This amazing shot is from the October 25, 1944 opening of the kamikaze offensive. In this case, a Zero-sen is diving on the escort carrier USS *White Plains* (CVE-66). Its attack demonstrated the difficulty inherent in crashing an aircraft onto a ship. The Zero-sen is approaching from the starboard quarter, but is in the process of turning right to hit the carrier. The aircraft missed the ship, but hit close aboard along the portside. The shock from the aircraft's exploding bomb was severe enough to force the carrier home for repairs. (NARA)

This A6M5 Zero-sen, carrying a 551lb bomb, is utilizing a dive profile against its target. When striking a ship, the most severe damage was caused by the explosion of the bomb, not by the impact of the aircraft. The absence of antiaircraft bursts around the Zero-sen suggests that it has surprised its target, which, in this case, was the carrier USS *Enterprise* (CV-6) on May 14, 1945. The ship was struck aft of the forward elevator and knocked out of the war. (via Jim Lansdale)

OPPOSITE

The IJNAF's primary kamikaze aircraft was the A6M5 Type 0 Model 52 fighter, which entered service in mid-1943. When employed in a suicide role, it could carry a Type 99 No. 25 Model 1 551lb bomb on its centerline via a specially fabricated rack, as seen here. Such a weapon greatly increased the Zero-sen's killing power as a kamikaze. This particular aircraft was one of more than 20 issued to the 205th Kokutai upon its formation at Taichung, on Formosa, on February 5, 1945. Pilots vastly outnumbered aircraft, with 112 naval aviators (mostly inexperienced cadets led by a core of 1st Air Fleet survivors from the Philippines) being on hand by March 10. With the 205th Kokutai's fundamental mission being kamikaze attacks, the unit moved to Ishigaki Shima and Miyako Shima, in the Ryukyu Island chain, when the battle for Okinawa commenced. Few aircraft were received by the 205th to replace those expended in suicide attacks, and by the end of May regular missions could no longer be sustained.

escorts. This was insufficient to inundate the CAP or a ship's antiaircraft defenses. By December 1944 attacks with larger groups of ten to twenty aircraft were common. By the Okinawa campaign, large waves of up to 50 aircraft were employed. These numbers were sufficient to saturate defenses and virtually guaranteed some aircraft would get through to the target.

Large groups of kamikazes would divide into smaller groups to enable them to approach the target from different directions, thus splitting the American CAP and defensive antiaircraft firepower. Evading the CAP was always the biggest problem. The most effective way to deal with the kamikaze threat was to intercept the suicide aircraft before they got anywhere near the target. This was difficult for the Americans to achieve on a consistent basis since there was never enough CAP available to cover all ships at all times.

Fighter pilots also faced significant problems while trying to execute a successful interception. When trying to detect targets near landmasses the radar picture seen aboard picket ships was often inconsistent, as shown on many occasions during the Philippines campaign. Even when detection was gained, it was difficult for most radar to provide an accurate altitude, which was essential for a successful interception. Later in the war the US Navy introduced the SP radar, which did provide reliable altitude information, making it a key technology to counter kamikazes.

The altitude issue meant that most CAPs would be flown at medium altitudes so that they could respond to Japanese aircraft at higher or lower altitudes. The Japanese quickly appreciated this, and approached targets at higher or lower altitudes to avoid the CAP. For a higher approach, the recommended altitude was 19,680–23,000ft – higher than the typical CAP altitude of 16,400ft. When a target was sighted, the kamikaze began a descent at 20 degrees to pick up speed and get through the CAP altitude as quickly as possible. When the pilot reached an altitude of 3,280–6,560ft, he would begin his attack dive at an angle of 45–55 degrees, taking the aircraft directly into the target. This was the approach recommended for lighter and faster aircraft such as the A6M Type 0 fighter. It had the advantage of being basic, and thus within the capabilities of inexperienced pilots. Such an attack was by no means simple though; the pilot still had to control the aircraft at high speed and in a steep dive, and then make the final adjustments to hit a moving target.

There was a second kamikaze attack approach that was even more challenging for the defender, but which took a greater degree of skill to fly. This was the low-altitude

A6M5 ZERO-SEN MODEL 52

29ft 11in.

205-142

11ft 6in.

36 1in.

In one of the iconic photographs of the Pacific War, a P1Y1 Navy Bomber Model 11 "Frances", already on fire, flies over the escort carrier USS *Ommaney Bay* (CVE-79) in the Sulu Sea on December 15, 1944. This aircraft missed, but on January 4, 1945, another "Frances" attacked *Ommaney Bay* without warning. Two perfectly placed bombs exploded in the ship, which destroyed all power and started a fire in the hangar that led to the carrier's loss. (NARA)

approach. This required the pilot to close on the target at 30–50ft off the deck. Within some 3,000ft of the target, the kamikaze would perform a "pop-up" maneuver to an altitude of 1,300–1,640ft to execute the final attack dive. To keep the target in sight during the terminal phase, the aircraft would conduct the final dive either partially or completely inverted. This was beyond the abilities of novice pilots. The low altitude approach had significant advantages. Most importantly, this approach profile brought the aircraft under the radar, which made detection and engagement by the CAP extremely difficult. It also posed problems for American antiaircraft gunners, since they often could not engage a target at that altitude without dramatically increasing the danger of hitting other ships in the formation.

By Okinawa the Japanese had settled on an attack profile that called for a high-speed, low-altitude attack from the beam. The low-altitude approach increased the likelihood of reaching the target area. While it was difficult to hit a target on the beam from a high-altitude dive, it was much easier from low altitude. A US Navy study calculated the difference was marked – only 17 percent of high-altitude kamikazes hit a beam target, but from a lower altitude, 67 percent did. The US Navy thought that this was the most effective attack profile.

The time of day was also important. Japanese attacks usually occurred at dawn and dusk when it was less likely for a CAP to be present.

Kamikaze pilots were also instructed to aim for certain parts of a ship. For an aircraft carrier, the most vulnerable points were the aircraft elevators and the island, where the command and control facilities were located. For other ships, the base of the bridge and the stack were considered the best aiming points. The most advantageous approach was from the stern for several reasons. The ship's antiaircraft defenses were weakest from this angle, it offered a better chance of a hit since the pilot had the full length of the ship to aim at, and it reduced the relative speed of the target. If a stern approach was not possible, then a bow approach was desired, since it also offered a weaker antiaircraft posture and gave the full length of the ship as a target. An approach from the beam was the most difficult, since it was into the teeth of the ship's defenses and offered only the narrow beam to hit.

When it came to the actual dive, the Japanese recognized that it was the natural tendency of the man in the cockpit to close his eyes before the crash. Therefore, pilots were instructed to keep their eyes open and to aim their aircraft until the moment of impact. The bravery of these young men was undoubted. They had to fly through blankets of antiaircraft fire and then fly themselves into a moving target. Many missed at the very last moment, probably because they flinched either as antiaircraft fire blossomed all around them or as a reaction to the mass of the ship rushing toward them just before impact.

In spite of all these tactics, which were the results of lessons learned, it was extremely difficult to effectively coordinate kamikaze attacks by inexperienced pilots in the face of well-trained US Navy fighter pilots and determined ships' gunners. US Navy observers reported that early attacks were mostly ill coordinated and were mounted by individual aircraft diving out of the clouds, which allowed the target ship to direct its full firepower at the single kamikaze. Later, during the Okinawa campaign, coordinated attacks were more likely, since larger groups of aircraft were being employed.

Another Japanese tactic used later in the war was the deployment of chaff to counter US Navy radars. When laid correctly, it had the potential to blind American radar operators.

The Japanese were able to refine their tactics because of US military intercepts of the reports of the kamikaze escorts. It was the responsibility of the escorts to provide protection from American CAPs and to report on the fate of each mission. Such

Vice Admiral Shigeru Fukudome (right), commander of land-based naval air forces in the Philippines, toasts his volunteers shortly before they depart on their suicide missions in late October 1944. Isolated from Japan and with few aircraft and no hope for survival, there was never any shortage of volunteers for kamikaze missions during the campaign in the Philippines. (via Henry Sakaida)

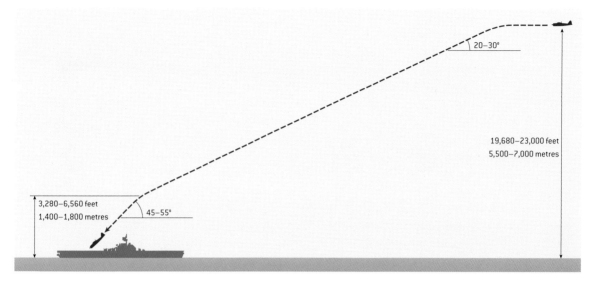

20–30°

19,680–23,000 feet
5,500–7,000 metres

3,280–6,560 feet
1,400–1,800 metres

45–55°

clouds

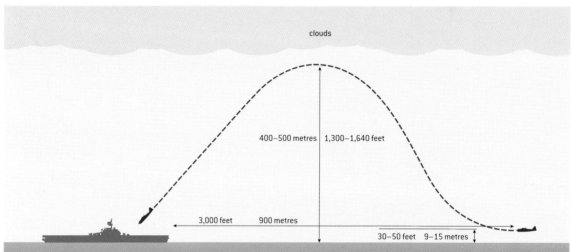

400–500 metres | 1,300–1,640 feet

3,000 feet | 900 metres

30–50 feet | 9–15 metres

These diagrams show the two most common kamikaze attack profiles. The high-altitude approach was the preferred profile for inexperienced pilots. More challenging for both the suicide pilot and the defender was a low-altitude approach, which, if flown low enough, could evade radar detection. Usually before executing his final dive, the low-altitude attacker would perform a pop-up maneuver to acquire a target. Occasionally, however, kamikazes would fly all the way to the target at low altitude.

reports allowed the Japanese to judge the effectiveness of kamikaze attacks and to analyze which tactics were successful and which were not.

Training for kamikaze missions also evolved. The first groups of volunteers in the Philippines were experienced pilots, so no training was required. These were quickly expended and new pilots with minimal experience took their place. Following the success of the first kamikaze attacks, Onishi had to train a larger pool of pilots to sustain his attacks. He came back with the promise of 150 reserve ensigns who, until recently, had been college students and who possessed fewer than 100 flying hours. Capt Rikihei Inoguchi, a staff officer assigned to Onishi's First Air Fleet, was assigned the task of turning students who could barely perform the basics of taking off and landing into pilots ready to conduct kamikaze attacks. His response was to create a seven-day course to make them kamikaze-ready. The first four days were spent on getting the basics down – taking off and flying in formation. The last three days were filled with approach and attack tactics.

OERLIKON 20mm CANNON

In this view, a 20mm cannon engages a Zero-sen fighter intending to crash on a US Navy carrier. The single mount is firing from the gun gallery on the deck edge of the carrier. The 20mm Oerlikon was the most-produced antiaircraft gun in US Navy history, with more than 88,000 being made. The US Navy adopted the Swiss-designed cannon in 1941 and the weapon had much to recommend it – a high rate of fire of 450 rounds per minute, an easily replaceable barrel and a high degree of reliability that made jamming unlikely. The weapon was air-cooled and ammunition was provided by detachable magazines that held 60 rounds. The mount did not require power, making it easy to place it anywhere with a clear firing arc.

Pointing and training was performed by the gunner using handlebars and shoulder rests. Guidance was originally provided by an open sight, and every fifth round was a tracer to aid spotting. In 1942, the open sight was gradually replaced by the Mk 14 gyro-stabilized gunsight, which dramatically increased the gun's effectiveness. All of this made the 20mm Oerlikon a capable weapon for engaging conventional attackers. However, the gun's 0.27lb projectile made it unsuited for engaging kamikazes.

THE US NAVY

The first requirement to defeat the kamikaze threat was detecting the oncoming suicide aircraft. This proved difficult for a number of reasons. The Japanese could take advantage of radar "shadows" caused by nearby land features, and they could also follow returning US Navy carrier aircraft back to their ships so closely that it was difficult for the sailors observing the radar plots to identify which aircraft were friendly and which were not. In the final approach, kamikazes could use cloud cover to conceal their attacks or dive out of the sun to blind gunners.

The inability of US Navy radar to provide adequate warning was a continuing and huge problem. The SK radar, the standard air-search system installed on larger ships, gave an uneven performance against both high- and low-flying aircraft. It could detect aircraft at distances well beyond 50 miles, only to lose them as they closed on the ship. If approaching at a lower altitude (below 15,000ft), the aircraft could be in a null void for 25 miles, during which time no radar in the task group could gain detection. This obviously made fighter direction virtually impossible. The SM radar was useful, but it had limited range at higher altitude. On large ships with both SK and SM radar, there was mutual interference that blocked out the latter system. When the kamikazes got near the task group the situation was even worse, with sea clutter and other radar signals making many systems useless.

ANTIAIRCRAFT TACTICS

There was a basic weakness in the US Navy's ability to defeat kamikaze attacks using ships' antiaircraft guns alone since the mainstay 20mm and 40mm guns were not powerful enough to destroy an incoming suicide aircraft. Both weapons were excellent in repelling conventional air attacks, however, and they exacted a heavy toll on Japanese aircraft engaged in such missions. Against suicide attacks they were found to be alarmingly ineffective. Even when these guns succeeded in setting an onrushing kamikaze on fire or knocking off a wing, the kinetic energy of the aircraft brought it toward the target and usually caused some damage, perhaps from a direct hit. In order to avoid damage, the kamikaze had to be destroyed or deflected far enough away from the ship so as to cause no damage.

The only weapon that held the prospects of destroying suicide aircraft far enough away from the ship to avoid damage was the ubiquitous 5in./38 dual-purpose gun mounted on many ships of destroyer-size and larger, or its earlier cousin the 5in./25 gun, which was carried on older cruisers and battleships. The fire control of these weapons was capable of hitting aircraft beyond 1,500 yards. Firing the Mk 32 proximity-fuze (VT – variable timing) shell greatly increased the effectiveness of the 5in. gun. Indeed, against kamikazes, Mk 32 shells were responsible for 56 percent of 5in./38 kills. The smaller 20mm and 40mm shells could not be fitted with a proximity fuze.

Although the 5in. VT round was the most effective in destroying suicide aircraft, it was also the least likely round to be fired at a kamikaze. This was because supplies of the Mk 32 VT round were always short. More importantly, the longer range of the 5in. gun was often left unused because the target was not picked up in time to allow an engagement at extended ranges. Thus, the smaller 20mm and 40mm guns remained the mainstay antiaircraft weapon.

A circular formation was the standard US Navy antiaircraft defensive tactic. It provided both defense in depth and all around protection, while still allowing the force to change directions easily. Maneuvering was also key to defeating the kamikaze, with experience showing that a ship at maximum speed with a continually changing course was best able to defeat an attack. The natural tendency of a ship's captain was to keep his beam to the kamikaze in order to generate the most antiaircraft power. However, as explained earlier in this chapter, beam attacks were deadly from low altitude, so the best maneuver would have been to make low-flying aircraft approach from the quarter and aircraft conducting a high-altitude dive to approach from the beam. A US Navy study also revealed that destroyers should not maneuver radically since it disrupted the effectiveness of their antiaircraft fire. On the other hand, large ships were advised to maneuver radically, since they were more stable gun platforms.

If the proper maneuvers were used, only 29 percent of kamikaze attacks were successful, but if they were not followed, 47 percent of dives were successful, according to the US Navy study.

NEW TACTICS AGAINST THE KAMIKAZE

By the final months of the war US Navy destroyers were being modified to increase their ability to operate in the face of the kamikaze threat. The torpedo battery was reduced or entirely removed from some ships and in its place extra radar and antiaircraft guns were fitted. In particular, picket destroyers were completed with SP radar installed.

The use of picket destroyers was increased during the Okinawa campaign when 15 stations were set up between 15–100 miles from the island. Each was manned by a destroyer and smaller supporting craft. At this point, pickets were not fitted with special radars but did embark fighter direction teams. In effect, they were acting as early warning radar platforms. The problem with this was that the pickets were too far apart to provide mutual protection, which in turn meant that they were vulnerable to mass kamikaze attack – losses on the picket stations were very heavy. This forced the US Navy to look for alternatives, all of which were still in the process of being evaluated as the war ended. These included using aircraft for early warning, submarines that could submerge when under kamikaze threat and more expendable destroyer escorts.

By the end of the war, the Fast Carrier Task Force had developed a doctrine in which it engaged incoming kamikazes at 12,000 yards using a high percentage of VT-fuzed shells. The task force was usually comprised of three task groups, which adopted a circular formation with the carriers in the middle. Destroyers were employed between the task groups to engage enemy aircraft attempting to fly between the American formations. Destroyers were also employed as pickets between the task force and enemy bases. These were not single pickets, but a division and even a squadron of destroyers. These ships played a vital role when it came to extending the early warning of an attack, providing fighter direction and helping prevent Japanese aircraft from tagging along with American aircraft returning to the task force. Each task group also developed procedures to enhance long-range antiaircraft fire.

TECHNICAL SPECIFICATIONS

A number of G4M2 "Betty" bombers were modified to carry the Ohka rocket bomb. This modification was designated the G4M2e Model 24J. With an Ohka onboard, the "Betty" was even more vulnerable than usual and proved an easy target for American fighters. Since the maximum range of the Ohka Model 11 was only 20 nautical miles, it was extremely problematic to fly a slow, ungainly "Betty" bomber within range of a target. Despite an insufficient number of escorting Zero-sen fighters, that was exactly what the 721st Kokutai Jinrai Butai (the Thunder God Corps) attempted to do on March 21, 1945 when it despatched 18 "Betty" bombers carrying the Ohkas to attack the American fleet. Here, the "Betty" crews sit waiting for the order to take off. (NHHC NH-73100)

KAMIKAZE AIRCRAFT

The IJNAF used many different types of aircraft as kamikazes. The preferred types were single-engined fighters and bombers because of their greater speed and higher

likelihood of penetrating American CAP screens and then executing a successful attack on a target. Nevertheless, twin-engined bombers were also used, including the IJNAF's vulnerable G4M "Betty" as both kamikazes and as carrier aircraft for the Ohka piloted rocket bomb. On occasion, various biplane floatplanes were also used.

The most numerous kamikaze aircraft by far was the A6M Type 0 Carrier Fighter. It was given the Allied reporting name "Zeke," but was most often referred to as the Zero-sen. This fighter was not only the most numerous IJNAF aircraft, it was well suited to the kamikaze role because of its obsolescence in aerial combat from the summer of 1944. Nevertheless, the Zero-sen possessed the speed and maneuverability to make it an excellent platform for suicide attacks. The aircraft also carried a 551lb bomb that proved more deadly than the kinetic power of the A6M itself when hitting a target.

The Zero-sen was originally designed as a carrier-based fighter. Having made its operational debut in 1940 over China, where the fighter proved superior to any opposing Allied type, the Zero-sen's success was due to its supreme maneuverability, which was made possible by its lightweight construction. The A6M2 Model 21 Zero-sen was superior to its early-war American counterparts, but it had begun to be

The MXY7 Navy Suicide Attacker Ohka ("Cherry Blossom") was developed as a piloted rocket bomb for suicide attack. With a top speed of 576mph, it could not be intercepted in a dive. Combined with a large 2,646lb Tekkou armor-piercing warhead, it appeared to be a weapon of great promise. (NARA)

The Ohka-carrying "Bettys" were sitting ducks for the Hellcats of VF-17 and VF-30 on March 21, 1945. Indeed, none of them returned from the mission. This gun camera film shows one of the bombers under attack, the wings of the Ohka being visible beneath the belly of the "Betty". (NARA 80G-185585)

The A6M5 Type 0 Carrier Fighter (commonly known as the Zero-sen) was by far the most common kamikaze aircraft. Although obsolescent by 1944 in its primary role as an air superiority fighter, its speed and maneuverability made it well suited for kamikaze attacks. (Peter M. Bowers Collection, Museum of Flight)

outclassed with the introduction of the F4U Corsair and the F6F Hellcat in 1943. The A6M quickly lagged behind in armament, pilot protection, higher-speed maneuverability and performance at altitude in comparison with more modern American fighters.

In response, the IJNAF introduced the A6M3 Model 32 from April 1942. This aircraft possessed a more powerful engine, but it produced only a marginal increase in performance. Because development of new aircraft to replace the Zero-sen was falling behind, the A6M was forced to soldier on as the primary IJNAF fighter. In August 1943, the next major variant of the Zero-sen was placed in production. This was the A6M5 Model 52, with an improved engine configuration and a new type of 20mm cannon. These modifications were insufficient to swing the balance against the latest American fighters, however, dooming the Zero-sen to increasing ineffectiveness in its primary role. The Japanese continued to introduce stopgap measures in the form of the A6M5a, A6M5b and A6M5c, which made incremental improvements in diving speed, armament, and protection, but this did not alter the balance of aerial superiority against the American fighters. Nevertheless, the A6M5 was effective in its new role as a suicide aircraft, providing the mainstay of the IJNAF's kamikaze operations for the remainder of the war.

One of the most prevalent kamikazes was the D3A2 Type 99 Carrier Bomber ("Val"). This view shows a Model 22 aircraft armed with a single 551lb Type 99 No. 25 Model 1 bomb on its centerline rack and single 140lb Type 99 No. 6 Model 1 weapons under each wing. It is being waved off on a suicide mission by groundcrew. (via Osamu Tagaya)

D3A2 Type 99 Model 22 Specification

Powerplant	1,100hp Kinsei 54
Dimensions	
Span	47ft 2in.
Length	33ft 5in.
Height	12ft 7in.
Wing area	376 sq ft
Weights	
Empty	5,666lb
Loaded	8,378lb
Performance	
Max Speed	267mph at 20,340ft
Range	840 miles
Rate of Climb	to 9,845ft in six minutes
Service Ceiling	34,450ft
Armament	Two 7.7mm Type 97 machine guns forward, one 7.7mm Type 92 rear-firing machine gun, one 551lb bomb, and two 132lb bombs

Representative of the attack aircraft used by the IJNAF in a kamikaze role was the D3A Type 99 Carrier Bomber. This aircraft was designed as a carrier-based dive-bomber and proved supremely effective in that role. Given the reporting name "Val" by the Allies, it was the standard carrier-based dive-bomber up until 1944. The "Val" was a very accurate dive-bomber, as shown by the fact that it accounted for more Allied ships than any other Japanese aircraft when used in a conventional role.

The aircraft looked antiquated with its fixed landing gear, and its resulting slow speed made the "Val" difficult to operate in contested airspace. In June 1942, an improved version with a more powerful engine began flight testing. The D3A2 Type 99 Carrier Bomber Model 22 began to replace the D3A1 from late 1942. The new

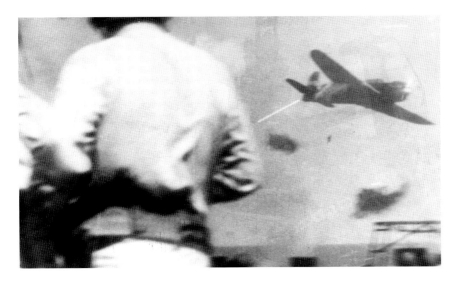

Among the many attack aircraft used by the IJNAF for kamikaze attacks was the B6N2 Carrier Attack Bomber (Allied reporting name "Jill"). Designed as a carrier-based aircraft to replace the B5N "Kate", it was capable of torpedo or bombing attacks. With a top speed of 299mph and the capability to carry a 1,764lb payload, the "Jill" was a capable kamikaze platform. (Getty Images)

A6M7 MODEL 63 COWLING GUN

Like the A5M5c Model 52c from which it was derived, the fighter/dive-bomber A6M7 Model 63 replaced the two ineffective 7.7mm Type 97 machine guns housed in the cowling of previous versions of the Zero-sen with a single 13.2mm Type 3 machine gun. The ammunition box for this weapon held 700 rounds.

variant possessed only a slight speed increase, however, and this did little to reduce the "Val's" increasing vulnerability. When the D4Y Carrier Bomber ("Judy") was introduced in 1943, the "Val" was reduced to secondary duties. From the autumn of 1944 land-based "Vals" were increasingly used as kamikaze aircraft, and in 1945 those examples previously assigned to training duties were brought back into frontline operation as suicide aircraft.

The JAAF also employed a wide range of aircraft for kamikaze missions, with older types that had been replaced by newer aircraft in frontline roles making up the bulk of the machines allocated to suicide missions. Predominant among these was the Ki-43 Army Type 1 Fighter. This was the most numerous JAAF fighter during World War II, with a total of almost 6,000 aircraft produced. Remaining in production through to the end of the war, it was given the reporting name "Oscar" by the Allies.

Development of the Ki-43 began in 1937 and emphasized maneuverability, but with a greater range and speed than the preceding Ki-27. Initial tests showed the Ki-43 to be little better than the fixed undercarriage Ki-27, and deliveries of the first

A6M7 MODEL 63 WING GUNS

The A6M7 Model 63's heavy punch was provided by two 20mm Type 99-2 cannons, one in each wing, supported by two more 13.2mm Type 3 machine guns outboard. Each of the latter weapons had a magazine housing 240 rounds, while the aircraft's belt-fed cannon had 100 rounds per gun.

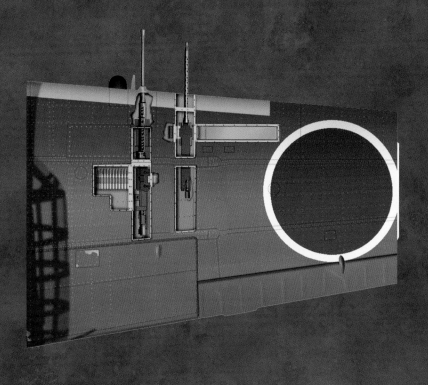

A6M5 Type 0 Model 52 Specification	
Powerplant	1,130hp Nakajima Sakae 21
Dimensions	
Span	36ft 1in
Length	29ft 11in.
Height	11ft 6in.
Wing area	229 sq ft
Weights	
Empty	4,136l
Loaded	6,025lb
Performance	
Max Speed	351mph at 19,685ft
Range	1,194 miles
Rate of Climb	to 19,685ft in seven minutes
Service Ceilin	38,520ft
Armament	Two 7.7mm Type 99 machine guns, two 20mm Type 99-2 cannons, and one 551lb bomb

The Ki-43 eventually became the most numerous JAAF kamikaze aircraft. After an uncertain start in the Philippines because of its unwillingness to commit experienced aircrew to suicide operations, the JAAF increased the scale of its kamikaze operations at Okinawa and by war's end was totally committed to the cause. In this famous photograph, taken on April 12, 1945, high school girls from Chiran, in Kagoshima Prefecture, wave farewell with cherry blossom branches to kamikaze pilot 2Lt Toshio Anazawa of the Army Special Attack Unit (20th Shinbu party). His aircraft is a Ki-43-III armed with a 551lb bomb.

Ki-43-IIIa Specification

Powerplant	1,150hp Army Type 1
Dimensions	
Span	35ft 7in.
Length	29ft 3in.
Height	10ft 9in.
Wing area	230 sq ft.
Weights	
Empty	4,233lb
Loaded	5,644lb
Performance	
Max Speed	358mph at 21,920ft
Range	1,990 miles
Rate of Climb	to 16,405ft in just over five minutes
Service Ceiling	37,400ft
Armament	two 12.7mm Type 1 (Ho-103) machine guns and one 551lb bomb

"Oscar" for squadron service did not occur until June 1941. The first model, the Ki-43-I was seen as an interim design, and work began immediately on the improved Ki-43-II, which became by far the most produced version. Despite early war success, the Ki-43-II was soon outclassed by its Allied rivals. Although the Japanese fighter was supremely maneuverable, it possessed an inferior top speed, a weak armament of only two 12.7mm machine guns and, like the Zero-sen, had little protection for its pilot or fuel tanks. In 1944 the improved Ki-43-III entered service, with a more powerful engine that increased the fighter's top speed. The aircraft's modest armament remained unchanged. When used as a kamikaze, the Ki-43-II and Ki-43-III could carry a 551lb bomb under the fuselage or wings.

THE US NAVY

The US Navy of 1944–45 was the largest naval force ever assembled. It was able to create an unparalleled mix of striking power in the form of its Fast Carrier Task Force and amphibious forces, supported by escorts and auxiliaries capable of keeping the fleet at sea for prolonged periods.

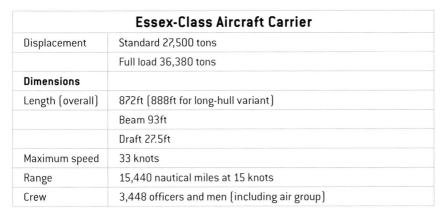

ESSEX-CLASS CARRIER

The iconic US Navy ship of the late-war period was the Essex-class fleet carrier. Twenty-four were built, and of these, 14 saw action during the Pacific War. These ships possessed a fine combination of speed, range, protection and unrivalled striking power in the form of a large air group. The lead ship, USS *Essex* (CV-9) was commissioned on December 31, 1942. By 1944, the Essex-class was the central element of the US Navy's drive to Japan.

The Essex-class carrier was the most formidable naval platform of the Pacific War. It was a fine mix of striking power, range, and defensive capabilities. This is USS *Yorktown* (CV-10), which was home to Carrier Air Group 9 during the Okinawa campaign. Much of the ship's carrier air group is spotted on the flightdeck aft. Although targeted numerous times by kamikaze aircraft, *Yorktown* was hit just once, on March 18, 1945. Unlike several of its sister-ships, the carrier only suffered minimal damage and remained fully operational. (NHHC)

Essex-class protection was excellent. An armored belt and a system of voids arranged along the hull provided protection against shells and torpedo attack. The flightdeck was

Essex-Class Aircraft Carrier	
Displacement	Standard 27,500 tons
	Full load 36,380 tons
Dimensions	
Length (overall)	872ft (888ft for long-hull variant)
	Beam 93ft
	Draft 27.5ft
Maximum speed	33 knots
Range	15,440 nautical miles at 15 knots
Crew	3,448 officers and men (including air group)

not armored since the weight required was prohibitive. The main armored deck was built into the hangar deck. The 2.5 inches of armor placed at the hangar deck level was calculated to be sufficient to stop large bombs from penetrating to the ship's vitals. Another 1.5 inches of armor was fitted on the fourth deck. The choice of non-armored flightdecks has been criticized, but the US Navy prioritized the provision of a large air group to maximize striking power. This required spacious and open hangar bays and would have been impossible if extensive armor had been fitted.

Essex-class carriers were provided with extensive antiaircraft suites. For long-range protection, 12 5in./38 guns were fitted – eight in twin mounts fore and aft of the island and four single mounts along the port side. Originally, eight 40mm quadruple mounts were also installed, and this number rose to a total of 18 on selected ships. Short-range protection was provided by 46 20mm single mounts placed on galleries

This is the Fletcher-class destroyer USS *Leutze* (DD-481) shown in April 1944. The ship is wearing a Measure 31, Design 16D camouflage scheme. Note the five 5in. single guns and the mid-war 40mm battery of five twin mounts. *Leutze* suffered a kamikaze attack on April 6, 1945 which inflicted extensive underwater damage that led to the destroyer being declared a constructive total loss. (NARA)

just below the flightdeck level. Some ships received as many as 58 of these guns. In 1945, in response to the kamikaze threat, a twin mount was introduced in place of the single mounts.

FLETCHER-CLASS DESTROYER

The destroyer was the most numerous principal surface combatant in the US Navy during the Pacific War. These ships were indispensable for a myriad of missions ranging from general escort and screening duties to anti-submarine warfare and air defense. They were used for missions where it was inadvisable to risk larger ships. This meant, for example, that when the US Navy decided to establish radar picket stations off Okinawa to provide more warning of approaching kamikazes, destroyers were the natural choice for the job. Their great numbers and assignment to exposed missions made them the most common target of kamikazes.

During the war the US Navy placed 287 destroyers into service. Of these, 175 were Fletcher-class ships, making this the most numerous class of destroyers in naval history. Almost all went to the Pacific, where they were used for everything from carrier screening to escorting amphibious forces and, eventually, radar picket duty.

Fletcher-Class	
Displacement	Standard 2,050 tons
	Full load 2,700 tons
Dimensions	
Length (overall)	376ft 6in.
	Beam 39ft 8in.
	Draft 22ft 8in.
Maximum speed	35 knots
Range	4,800 nautical miles at 15 knots
Crew	273 officers and men

A6M7 MODEL 63 CENTERLINE 551LB BOMB

The more powerful A6M5 and A6M7 models of the Zero-sen could carry ordnance weighing up to 1100lb on a single centerline rack. Typically, however, the aircraft would be armed with a single Type 99 No. 25 Model 1 551lb bomb, as seen here. The body of this weapon consisted of one piece of machined forged steel three-quarters of an inch in thickness. It was threaded in the nose to receive a fuze. The after end of the body was threaded internally to accommodate a male base plate. The latter was drilled centrally to receive the tail fuze. The weapon's tail cone was secured to the base plate by six screws. Four fins were welded to the tail cone and braced by a single set of box-type struts. The bomb body was filled with Type 91 (trinitroanisol) explosive. Designed in 1938 and adopted by the IJNAF the following year, the Type 99 No. 25 Model 1 bomb was capable of penetrating 50mm of armor before exploding.

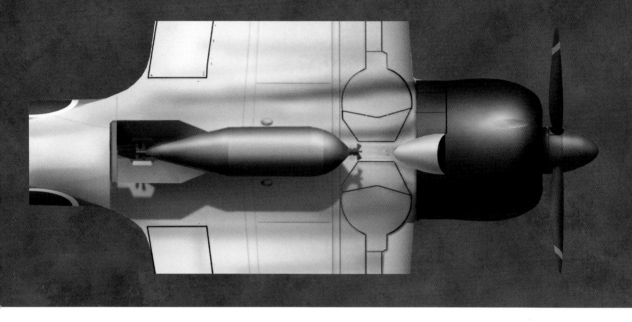

Design of the new destroyer class was based on earlier 1,630-ton destroyers. To carry the desired five 5in./38 guns and ten torpedo tubes, the new class was expanded to more than 2,000 tons and the ship's length extended by 28ft 6in. This increased size reduced the maximum speed, but it did allow for a much more balanced design

Seen here in 1942, USS *Fletcher* (DD-445) was the lead ship of the Fletcher-class destroyers, 175 of which were commissioned between 1942 and 1944. The mainstay of the US Navy's Pacific campaign, the Fletcher-class destroyers, like all early-war American warships, possessed inadequate antiaircraft capabilities. These required constant improvement during the war. (NARA)

that had good capabilities in anti-submarine, anti-surface and, most importantly by 1944–45, anti-air warfare. The class was also able to accommodate wartime modifications that proved to be important when its radar and antiaircraft fit was upgraded. All ships carried a standard battery of five 5in./38 guns in single mounts. The light antiaircraft gun fit was continually upgraded throughout the war. The standard 1942–43 fit was a twin 40mm mount and six single 20mm mounts. By 1943 and into early 1945, most ships carried five twin 40mm mounts and seven 20mm single guns. In response to the kamikaze threat and the imperative to mount more 40mm guns, in 1945 some ships carried 14 40mm guns in two quadruple and three twin mounts and 12 20mm guns in six twin mounts.

US NAVY SHIPBOARD ANTIAIRCRAFT WEAPONS

Most larger US Navy ships carried three types of antiaircraft guns. The longest-range weapons were medium-caliber guns, and in the US Navy this was epitomized by the 5in./38 dual-purpose gun. Intermediate-range weapons such as the 40mm gun provided the next layer of defense. Finally, every ship carried a number of short-range weapons, almost always the 20mm gun, to provide close-in defense.

The effective ranges of these weapons varied. A four-gun 5in./38 battery under director control was effective to 10,000 yards while a 5in./25 could reach 7,000 yards. Director-controlled 40mm guns were effective to 3,000 yards and the 20mm with the Mk 14 sight was effective to as much as 2,000 yards. The 5in./25 gun was installed in older cruisers, battleships and carriers, its design dating back to 1921. It had a short barrel to make it easier to engage fast targets, but this also gave it a fairly low velocity and thus a reduced range.

The follow-on to the 5in./25 was the 5in./38, which was a very successful design that became the US Navy's standard dual-purpose gun of World War II. Indeed, it was the most successful gun of its type during the conflict. Increasing the barrel length increased muzzle velocity and thus ceiling. Firing semi-fixed ammunition, the hand-operated but power-rammed gun achieved a high rate of fire – a well-trained crew could fire 15 rounds per minute or more.

For the 5in. gun, fire control was a very difficult issue. To be effective, it had to accurately predict where a target would be moving in three dimensions and then place a properly fuzed shell close enough to it to do damage. Rangefinders were key to finding

The US Navy's 5in./38 dual-purpose gun with its large shell offered the best chance of defeating a kamikaze before it could damage a target. These are the forward twin mounts on *Intrepid*. (NHHC)

Principal US Navy Antiaircraft Guns				
Weapon	Muzzle velocity (feet/sec)	Ceiling (feet)	Shell weight (pounds)	Rate of fire (rounds per minute, theoretical)
5in./25	2,110	27,400	52	14
5in./38	2,600	37,200	54	15–20
40mm	2,890	22,800	2	160
20mm	2,740	10,000	.27	450

target location, but were subject to inherent inaccuracies. The key to producing an effective fire solution was using the measurements from the rangefinder to produce the rate at which the range changed. Once calculated, and the longer the time of measurement the greater the accuracy, then a prediction could be made as to where the target would be to produce deflections to aim the gun. The Mk 33 fire-control system was the first built to control the new 5in./38 gun. It was installed in older destroyers, heavy cruisers and a few carriers. The Mk 33 was self-contained with its own rangefinder. With power drive, it could handle targets traveling at speeds up to 320 knots and also had a mode to handle an aircraft diving at 400 knots. In action, the Mk 33 proved too slow to generate target solutions, especially against a maneuvering target.

The US Navy's standard intermediate-range antiaircraft weapon was the Swedish-designed 40mm Bofors gun. This was the best weapon of its type during the war and it had a solid record of being able to successfully engage conventional air attacks. Against the kamikaze, however, the 40mm gun lacked the hitting power to be entirely successful. (NARA)

Effectively the JAAF's A6M Zero-sen equivalent, the Ki-43 "Oscar" was available in large numbers during the doomed campaigns fought in defense of the Philippines and Okinawa. One of the units rushed to the Philippines following the American landings was the 20th Hiko Sentai, which flew to Caloocan airfield, near Manila, from Formosa on October 22, 1944. This aircraft of the unit's 1st Chutai was among the 18 Ki-43-IIs sent to Caloocan, and on November 1 it was sent to Fabrica airfield, on Negros Island, to join the battle over Leyte. Most of the 20th Hiko Sentai's pilots were inexperienced, yet they were thrown straight into action. They duly suffered terrible losses attempting to escort JAAF suicide attackers flying Ki-48 bombers against US Navy ships in Leyte Gulf. Eventually, the Hiko Sentai was also ordered to expend its surviving Ki-43s and pilots in kamikaze strikes, configuring the "Oscars" as depicted here – with a 551lb Type 92 high explosive bomb beneath the left wing and a 200-liter drop tank beneath the right wing, the latter being carried both to extend the fighter's range and to offset the weight of the weapon.

The ultimate fire control system for the 5in./38 was the Mk 37. This new system had a small director topside and its computers below decks. This was the standard medium-range fire control system on all wartime ship construction. The system could automatically generate solutions on targets moving at 400 knots horizontally and 250 knots diving. The effectiveness of the system was enhanced with the integration of radar. The first radar to be incorporated was the Mk 4, which reduced the time required to generate a target solution.

The Mk 37 was not perfect, and by 1945 was showing its weakness in the face of the kamikazes. It was best beyond 6,000 yards, but was increasingly less accurate into 3,000 yards, and very inaccurate in closer than 300 yards. This led to a common late-war practice of using the Mks 51 and 57 manual directors at close range. A number of ships split their 5in. battery, with some controlled by the Mk 37 for better long-range fire, and others with the manual directors for close-in work. With guns half-loaded and the system set for a diving attack, fire could be opened in a second or less.

The effectiveness of the 5in. gun was greatly increased by the introduction of the proximity fuze, which the US Navy called the VT (variable timing) fuze for security reasons. It was the result of a high-priority and highly classified research effort begun in 1940 to develop a fuze small enough to fit in a 5in. shell that could send out radio signals to detect the presence of a target. This removed the problem of having to pre-set a fuze with the range at which the target was predicted to be. It also greatly increased the effectiveness of the 5in. gun as an antiaircraft weapon, making it effective at short ranges. The US Navy estimated that a VT-fuzed round was four times more effective than a regular shell.

For the 40mm gun, fire control was initially provided by the Mk 44 director, which was essentially a dummy weapon that took three men to operate. This was eventually replaced by the less complex and more effective Mk 51. The latter was essentially a Mk 14 gyro-sight on a pedestal. Because the Mk 51 was placed away from the vibration, smoke and flash of a gun, it was much more effective. The Mk 51 was hand-slewed, so it could respond to surprise attacks. It also generated a fire-control solution more quickly than other systems. Finally, the Mk 51 was simple to produce, which meant that it could be fitted in large numbers. The Mk 51 provided training and elevation commands to the mount, which were then executed by electric power. Late in the war the Mk 51 was replaced by the Mks 57 and 63 directors. These were the first directors for automatic weapons to offer blind-fire capabilities.

Guidance for the short-range 20mm gun was simpler, with the weapon firing tracer rounds that the gunner guided via a ring sight that could be used at standard ranges for aircraft moving at different speeds. The gun could also be paired with a Mk 14 gyro-sight, which the US Navy estimated made the 20mm cannon 50 percent more effective than when the gunner relied on the sight and tracers method. The Mk 14 was designed to handle a 200-knot target, but it proved reasonably accurate against aircraft flying at 500 knots.

Late in the war the US Navy began to replace single 20mm mounts with twin 20mm mounts. This increased firepower and saved some weight, thus compensating for the additional weight from the increased numbers of 40mm guns mounted on many ships.

Ki-43-II "OSCAR"

29ft 3in.

10ft 9in.

35ft 7in.

Even more than the 40mm Bofors gun, the US Navy's standard light antiaircraft gun, the 20mm Oerlikon, was ineffective against kamikazes, since its projectiles were unable to break up incoming aircraft. (NARA)

Data collected by the US Navy showed that the vast majority of kamikaze kills were scored by 20mm and 40mm automatic weapons. The totals were 50 percent by 40mm, 27 percent by 20mm, and the remainder accounted for by 5in./38 guns. This brought to the fore a critical problem – automatic weapons fired too small a projectile to break up incoming suicide aircraft. Nevertheless, the 40mm gun was the most effective in shooting down kamikazes, which explains why the US Navy expended so much effort in increasing the numbers of these weapons fitted to ships of destroyer-size and larger. The 20mm weapon was not viewed as an effective counter to the kamikaze, since it had a short engagement range. Furthermore, even if rounds from the gun struck the target, the kamikaze often still succeeded in hitting the ship.

By this late stage in the war, most US Navy combatants had some sort of combat information center (CIC) with which to fuse target data and assign them to the ship's weapons. CICs were still fairly primitive, however, and they could be swamped by anything more than a limited number of raids, especially when it came to directing fighters. When the incoming Japanese aircraft split into smaller groups, the CIC was easily saturated.

THE STRATEGIC SITUATION

By mid 1944, the Pacific War had taken a dramatic turn against the Japanese. The first major naval engagement since late 1942 had just been fought in June 1944 off the Mariana Islands. The result was not the victory that the Japanese had planned for, but instead a decisive defeat for the IJN. The rebuilt Japanese carrier force was dealt a stinging blow, with three of the nine carriers engaged being sunk and, more importantly, almost all of the IJNAF carrier aircraft committed to the battle being destroyed and their crews lost. This defeat crippled the Japanese carrier force for the remainder of the war. By August the Marianas were in American hands, which meant that B-29 bombers were now only 1,200 miles from Japan – close enough to strike the homeland.

The American high command had some difficulty in determining its next target following the occupation of the Marianas. The forces under Admiral Chester Nimitz had the Palau Islands targeted for a September 15 landing, while the Southwest Pacific forces under General Douglas MacArthur were planning to land on Mindanao, in the Philippines, on November 15. Nimitz and his US Navy boss Admiral Ernest King had a different view from that of MacArthur on how best to achieve the goal of seizing bases leading to a direct attack on Japan. While MacArthur wanted to re-conquer the Philippines first, the US Navy proposed to bypass that country after the initial landings on Mindanao in favor of an attack on Formosa and seizing a base on the coast of China. Either way, the capture of the Philippines or Formosa would cut Japan off from the resources-rich areas of the Netherlands East Indies. Without the flow of raw materials from the south, Japan could not effectively continue the war.

MAP OVERLEAF

The Japanese first employed kamikazes in their defense of the Philippines from October 1944 through to January 1945. Initial attacks concentrated on US Navy forces located in Letye Gulf and to the east. In December the US Navy moved into Ormoc Bay, to the west of Leyte, and immediately came under kamikaze attack. Moving through the Sulu Sea, the Americans landed on Mindoro on December 15. This invasion force was also subjected to an intense kamikaze reaction. The heaviest suicide attacks of the campaign, however, came against the US Navy's large invasion fleet undertaking the amphibious landings on Luzon in January 1945. For ten days ships of the US Navy were subjected to concerted suicide attack as they entered Lingayen Gulf. The last attacks of the campaign were conducted on January 13, after which the IJNAF and JAAF ran out of aircraft.

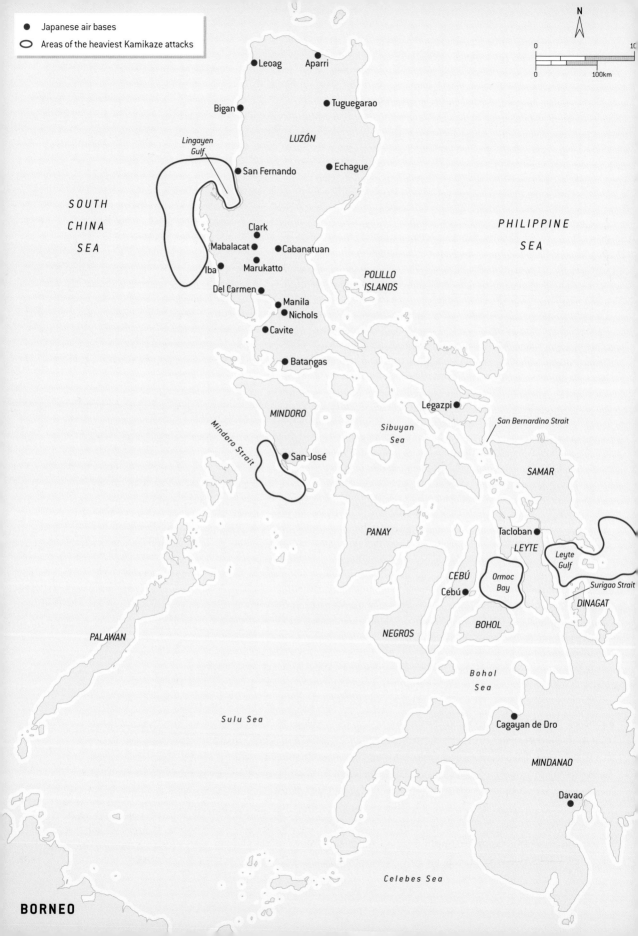

N

0   10
0   100km

Leoag

Aparri

Bigan

Tuguegarao

LUZÓN

Lingayen Gulf

San Fernando

Echague

SOUTH CHINA SEA

Clark

Mabalacat

Cabanatuan

Iba

Marukatto

Del Carmen

Manila

Nichols

Cavite

Batangas

PHILIPPINE SEA

POLILLO ISLANDS

MINDORO

Mindoro Strait

San José

Legazpi

San Bernardino Strait

Sibuyan Sea

SAMAR

PANAY

Tacloban

LEYTE

Leyte Gulf

CEBÚ

Cebú

Ormoc Bay

Surigao Strait

DINAGAT

NEGROS

BOHOL

PALAWAN

Bohol Sea

Sulu Sea

Cagayan de Dro

MINDANAO

Davao

Celebes Sea

BORNEO

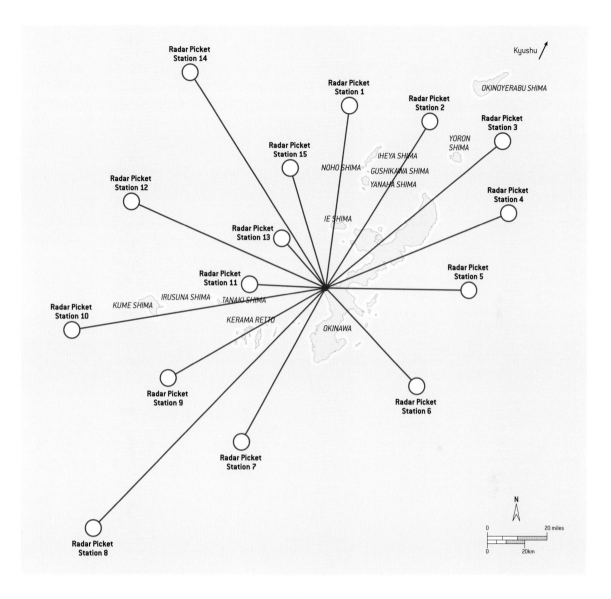

Events in China beginning in May 1944 made the King–Nimitz plan untenable. A major Japanese offensive cut Chinese forces off from the coast, making the plan to develop a base on the mainland unrealistic. A meeting in Hawaii on July 26–27, 1944 between President Franklin D. Roosevelt, Nimitz and MacArthur endorsed the General's plan to land on Mindanao on November 15, followed by Leyte, in the central Philippines, on December 20. But this timetable did not survive long. During a series of carrier raids on the Philippines to prepare for the invasion, Admiral William Halsey, commander of the Third Fleet, encountered such weak opposition that on September 13 he proposed that the Mindanao landings be canceled and an immediate invasion of Leyte be made instead. This suggestion found favor with all parties, and MacArthur's staff came up with a new landing date for Leyte – October 20.

Unlike MacArthur's earlier amphibious operations on New Guinea, which were executed within range of friendly air bases, the planned landing on Leyte would be conducted without the benefit of supporting airfields in the southern Philippines. Air cover for the operation would be provided by the fleet carriers of Task Force (TF) 38 of the Third Fleet. Assisting them with air cover for the invasion fleet were the escort carriers of the Seventh Fleet. As soon as possible, air bases on Leyte would be developed to take the strain off TF 38. In the event, the monsoon weather from October to December and the unstable soil on Leyte combined to delay airfield construction. This required the carriers to remain on station well beyond the planned time, making them vulnerable to Japanese air attack since they were tied down to a specific geographic area.

As the Americans pondered their next move, the Japanese had no difficulty in ascertaining that the Philippines was the next objective for US forces in the western Pacific. Since the Philippines controlled the vital sea lanes running from the South China Sea to Japan, Imperial General Headquarters decided to fight for it with all available forces. This would include an effort by virtually all remaining warships of the IJN to attack the American beachhead. Supporting this attack were the land-based air forces of the IJNAF's Second Air Fleet on Formosa and Kyushu and the First Air Fleet in the Philippines.

The Japanese plan for defending the Philippines offered no real prospects for success, having two fatal flaws. Because the Japanese were uncertain as to the precise place and time of the American invasion, the IJN could not activate its forces until the location of the landings had been confirmed. This meant that the October 20 landings on Leyte were initially unopposed. Five days would pass before the IJN could arrive off Leyte with naval forces, by which time the Americans were well established ashore. The second fatal flaw was that the Japanese were devoid of strong air forces. Any hope they had of mounting serious air attacks on the US Navy's invasion force was ended after the October 12–14 aerial battle off Formosa, during which the Third Fleet accounted for some 500 Japanese aircraft. No significant damage was inflicted on the Third Fleet in return.

The series of engagements known collectively as the Battle for Leyte Gulf were so disastrous for the Japanese that it spelled the end of the IJN as an effective fighting force. It was during this battle that the kamikaze made their first appearance, and by the end of it they constituted Japan's most viable option for responding to the invasion of Leyte and future American targets in the Philippines and beyond.

The battle opened on October 24 with an all-day assault by TF 38 on the main IJN force (the First Diversionary Attack Force) assigned to attack the beachhead on Leyte. More than 250 sorties were flown against this force of battleships and heavy cruisers, which had no air cover. The American strikes sunk the superbattleship *Musashi* and damaged the heavy cruiser *Myoko* so badly that it was forced to retire.

Japanese air power had been directed at TF 38 to pave the way for this force, these conventional air attacks enjoying limited success with the destruction of the light carrier USS *Princeton* (CVL-23). Overall, however, they were ineffective in protecting the passage of the main Japanese force. The following day, the First Diversion Attack Force transited through the San Bernardino Strait and headed south to Leyte. East of Samar it ran into the Seventh Fleet's escort carrier force. In a confused action, the heavier Japanese force, still containing four battleships and six heavy cruisers plus escorts, was harried by the aircraft from 12 escort carriers and bravely attacked by US Navy destroyers and destroyer escorts. When the Japanese broke off the action, only the escort carrier USS *Gambier Bay* (CVE-73) from a task group named "Taffy 3" had been sunk. In return, the IJN lost three heavy cruisers and any chance of achieving a Pyrrhic victory by entering Leyte Gulf and attacking the American beachhead. Later that morning "Taffy 1" and Taffy "3" came under suicide attack, opening the era of the kamikaze in the Pacific War.

The remainder of the battle was even more disastrous for the IJN. The force assigned to enter Leyte Gulf from the south was annihilated with the loss of two battleships, a heavy cruiser, and three destroyers. The IJN's hollow carrier force, acting as a decoy to allow the passage of the First Diversion Attack Force into Leyte Gulf, came under heavy American carrier air attack and lost all four of its carriers. Total Japanese losses during the battle were four carriers, three battleships, six heavy cruisers, four light cruisers and 11 destroyers.

The demise of the IJN meant that only air units were left to disrupt the American drive to land on the main island of Luzon in January 1945. As we shall see, the most effective component of Japanese air attacks was the kamikaze. Following the landings on Luzon, the next American objective was on the doorstep of Japan. The occupation of Okinawa, which lay roughly 300 miles south of Japan, was critical in order to seize bases for the subsequent invasion of the home islands. The Japanese were determined to exact a high toll from the invaders to demonstrate that the cost to invade Japan would be greater than the Americans were willing to pay. The Okinawa campaign from April to June 1945 featured the most intense kamikaze attacks yet, and put the US Navy to the supreme test.

Its invasion force had to remain near the island for weeks and eventually months, giving the enemy the perfect opportunity to mount sustained kamikaze attacks. The Japanese objective was to force the invasion fleet to leave the waters off Okinawa. More likely would be a demonstration that the cost of mounting an invasion in the face of a sustained kamikaze threat would be too costly, possible throwing the planned attack on Japan proper into doubt. Either way, the kamikaze was the last resort open to the Japanese Empire to avoid total defeat.

The most severe challenge faced by US Navy carriers during the war was the kamikaze. Essex-class ships suffered 13 successful kamikaze attacks, but none were sunk. This is *Intrepid* on November 25, 1944, the ship being hit on three occasions by kamikazes – the most of any US Navy carrier. (NHHC)

THE COMBATANTS

PSYCHE OF THE KAMIKAZE

Most kamikaze pilots were between 20 and 25 years old. Many were highly educated university students and all were volunteers, although the nature of their volunteering for suicide missions was done in many ways. It would be difficult to imagine a young Japanese man not conforming to the expectation that he volunteer for whatever mission his superiors believed as necessary and deny the social pressures to conform to the notion that every Japanese patriot would expend his life, if necessary, to defend the nation.

The initial batches of kamikaze pilots were formed in the Philippines from established units. The men in these units, many battle-experienced, had seen how ineffective conventional tactics had become against the growing strength of the American fleet. It is perhaps not surprising that many of them volunteered as kamikazes in the belief that their deaths could bring a greater return than dying ineffectively in conventional attacks. The usual image of a kamikaze pilot is that of a young draftee who was given only minimal training, and then volunteered to fly a suicide mission. Although it differed by unit, some measures were taken to ensure that men were in fact volunteering to die. There are no known instances where pilots were ordered to fly a suicide mission against their will. This would not even have been necessary since there were many more volunteers than there were aircraft available.

The motivations of kamikaze pilots were basically simple. On the surface, these men wanted to conform to expectations from their fellow aviators, their family, and

USS *INTREPID* (CV-11)

These artworks depict the Essex-class aircraft carrier USS *Intrepid* (CV-11) as it appeared on November 25, 1944 when the ship was hit for the first of several times by kamikazes. *Intrepid* ended the war with the dubious distinction of having endured more kamikaze attacks than any other US Navy carrier. The ship has been painted in the distinctive MS-32/3A dazzle camouflage adopted by the US Navy following research by the Naval Research Laboratory. Using a mix of obtrusive patterns on vertical surfaces in Light Gray, Ocean Gray and Dull Black, the dazzle scheme was applied in order to make it difficult for the enemy to estimate the ship's heading, speed and range. Each ship's dazzle pattern was also unique so as to make it more difficult for the enemy to recognize different classes of ship.

Pilots from the JAAF's 72nd Shinbu-tai pose for the camera on May 26, 1945. Three of the five aviators are 17 years old and the other two are 18 and 19. They are, from left to right in the front row, Tsutomu Hayakawa, Yukio Araki, and Takamasa Senda, with Kaname Takahashi and Mitsuyoshi Takahashi behind them. Flying Ki-51 "Sonias", all five pilots were killed on May 27 when they attacked US Navy radar picket ships including the destroyer USS *Braine* (DD-630). The latter was hit twice, killing 66 sailors and wounding 78. Although badly damaged, the ship survived and was subsequently repaired post-war.

from Japanese society. Many, and probably most, were also guided by a spirit of sacrifice to defend the nation. Many felt an obligation to repay their family and the nation by giving their lives.

The notion that these men were robots who performed their last duties without regret is incorrect. Ultimately, all were volunteers, although subtle coercion was undoubtedly a part of the process. There was no great overt pressure placed on men to volunteer. They were not brainwashed into crashing their aircraft against American ships. Many left behind thoughtful letters explaining their choice and expressing their hope that their sacrifice would display the moral strength that Japan would need to deal with the desperate situation it was in and with the likelihood of rebuilding the nation after defeat.

Given the pure motives of the kamikaze pilots, and the ultimately futile nature of their sacrifice, it is easy to blame their superiors for cynically leading them to suicide. For their part, they were making a cold calculation that conventional attacks were fruitless and that the only prospects for success were special attacks. Of course, the proper conclusion that should have been reached by late 1944 was that continuing the war was hopeless. The allure of suicide attacks, which would give the Americans another example of the purity of the Japanese spirit and perhaps a reason to re-think paying the necessary price to achieve total victory, gave Japan's leaders an irresponsible reason to continue the war. The same leaders who went to war with no real idea of how to conclude it successfully were now content to oversee the total destruction of the nation. The kamikaze pilots paid a dramatic part, but a very small part, in this final period of shortsightedness by Japan's reckless leaders.

THE KAMIKAZE AND THE US NAVY SAILOR

Part of the intent of the kamikaze was to produce a weapon of terror. It has to be admitted that the employment of such a weapon so foreign to the Western mentality did have a dramatic impact on the typical American sailor. To every sailor under attack, it looked like the kamikaze bearing down relentlessly on his ship was aiming directly at him. The only way to deal with this threat was to destroy the aircraft before it hit the ship. The initial realization that the Japanese were using human bombs to hit their ship left many sailors dumbfounded and led to a brief loss of confidence.

American sailors dealt with this reality in different ways. The most common method was to dismiss it as crazy, something that they could not understand, and deal with the fear. Some derided kamikazes as cowardly, but this was obviously untrue as the kamikazes took a growing toll. Some of the observers admired it for what it was – an act of desperate courage.

The toll exacted on the American sailors forced to deal with this new and deadly threat was high, both in physical and psychological terms. The kamikaze threat

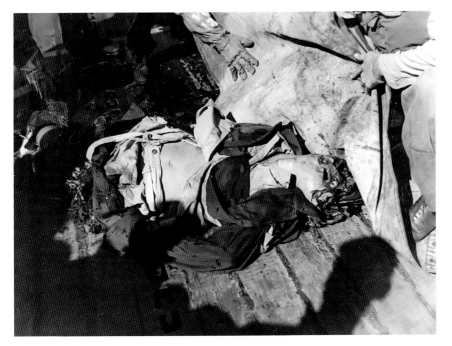

The body of the suicide pilot who crashed into *Intrepid* on November 25, 1944. In this case, the sacrifice of one suicide pilot and his aircraft cost the US Navy 64 killed and 35 wounded and forced the ship out of combat until March 1945. (NARA)

required a new level of constant awareness. Ships in danger areas were on constant alert, with crews at battle stations or close to their battle stations since there was often little warning of an attack. Too often, the first indication of an attack was the visual report of a Japanese aircraft directly overhead making its final dive. The threat seemed to be random – some ships were singled out for attention while others nearby were ignored. Usually, the ship's antiaircraft guns were able to engage the target, but here

The human cost of the kamikaze offensive is depicted in this image. When *Essex* came under attack on November 25, 1944, the suicide aircraft crashed inboard from the aft port 20mm gun galleries. One of the guns was manned by six stewards who served their weapon until the last moment and were all killed. One of the undercarriage legs from the kamikaze aircraft can be seen at the top of the photograph. (NARA)

43

A contemporary news photograph purporting to show an Army Special Attack Unit composed of recently trained university students taking their Ki-43-III fighters to the front in the spring of 1945. These machines are each equipped with two 200-liter drop tanks and no bombs, which does indeed suggest that the "Oscar" pilots were setting out on a flight to their new frontline bases, rather than a one-way suicide mission. (via Edward M. Young)

The cost to the US Navy was high every time a suicide aircraft hit a ship. The average number of casualties caused by a successful kamikaze attack was 40. In this view, some of the 15 crewmen killed onboard *Essex* on November 25, 1944 are being buried at sea the following day. It was common practice to bury men at sea if they were killed in action. (NARA)

again the disturbing nature of the threat came to light. If hit by a 5in. shell, the suicide aircraft would disintegrate. If engaged by smaller weapons, even the standard 40mm gun, the kamikaze was often seen to be hit by multiple rounds but refused to go down. The aircraft could be seen shedding parts as the antiaircraft shells impacted, but it would continue remorselessly to its target.

When the scope of the new threat was evident, which came after the initial shock of the introduction of the kamikaze during the Leyte campaign and when attacks increased in the lead-up to the invasion of Luzon, the US Navy's leadership placed censorship rules to prevent the spread of the news of the kamikaze threat. This was done primarily to deny the Japanese any information on the effectiveness of their new weapon, but it also had the effect of dampening the psychological impact of the suicide attacks within the US Navy and at home. Sailors returning to the United States or enjoying leave in Australia were told not to talk about the new threat, and their mail was also censored to delete any similar mention. Of course, such a blackout was impossible to maintain. The news embargo was lifted on April 12, 1945.

Through the entire ordeal, the strain on the men facing the kamikazes increased to new levels, especially during the Okinawa campaign when large waves of suicide aircraft were employed by the Japanese. At no time did the kamikaze threat break the morale of the men facing them, however, the US Navy proving able to deal with the largest threat it faced during the war and still conduct its mission of tightening the stranglehold around Japan.

A6M5C/7 ZERO-SEN COCKPIT

1. Type 98 reflector gunsight
2. Artificial horizon
3. Turn and bank indicator
4. 13.2mm Type 3 machine gun
5. High altitude automatic mixture control
6. Exhaust temperature gauge
7. Clock
8. Airspeed indicator
9. Magnetic compass
10. Rate of climb indicator
11. Fuel and oil pressure gauge
12. Tachometer
13. Emergency fuel pump lever
14. Direction finder control unit
15. Emergency power boost
16. Radio direction indicator
17. Magneto switch
18. Altimeter
19. Control column
20. Manifold pressure gauge
21. Oil temperature gauge

22. Cylinder head temperature gauge
23. Cockpit light
24. Throttle quadrant/20mm Type 99-2 cannon firing lever
25. Primer
26. Oxygen supply gauge
27. Hydraulic pressure gauge
28. 20mm Type 99-2 cannon master switch
29. Oil cooler shutter control
30. Cowl flap control
31. Radio control unit
32. Elevator trimming tab control

33. Circuit breakers
34. Rudder pedals
35. Wing tanks cooling air intake control
36. Emergency gear down lever
37. Loop antenna handle
38. Seat up/down lever
39. Fuel tank jettison handle
40. Fuselage tank fuel gauge
41. Wing tanks fuel gauge
42. Emergency fuel jettison lever
43. Fuselage/wing tanks switching cock
44. Wings tank selector lever
45. Bomb release levers
46. Seat
47. Arresting hook winding wheel
48. Wing tank fuel switching cock

COMBAT

War-weary A6M3 Zero-sens armed with 551lb bombs, escorted by drop tank-equipped A6M5s, taxi out at Davao, on Mindanao Island, on October 25, 1944 to signal the start of the kamikaze campaign. After several aborted attempts over previous days, during which no targets were found, the first successful kamikaze attacks took place on this date when the escort carriers of "Taffy 1" and "Taffy 3" were hit hard. (*via Henry Sakaida*)

ADVENT OF THE KAMIKAZE

After Onishi arrived in the Philippines, he wasted no time in establishing the first kamikaze unit. Comprised of 24 pilots and ready for action on October 20, it was divided into four sub-units. After several aborted attempts during which no targets were found, the first successful kamikaze attacks had to wait until October 25. Mounted by a handful of aircraft, it was a smashing success.

October 25 was also the climactic day of the Battle of Leyte Gulf, when the main IJN surface force fell upon the US Navy's escort carriers east of Samar. The later were organized into three groups. "Taffy 3" was the group that came under Japanese surface attack, while "Taffy 1" to the south had the dubious distinction of being the first US Navy formation to be targeted by kamikazes.

Six suicide aircraft, all Zero-sens, took off with escorts from Davao, on Mindanao Island, and headed north. They soon spotted "Taffy 1" with its four escort carriers and escorting ships. Although detected by American radar, the aircraft were not spotted as they approached the US Navy formation

A group of Japanese aircraft above the escort carriers St. Lo and Kitkun Bay on October 25, 1944. The sailors onboard these ships could not know that this was no conventional attack, but the beginning of a whole new phase of the war. (NARA)

through scattered clouds. The first attack was directed at the escort carrier USS *Santee* (CVE-29) at 0740 hrs. Surprise was complete, and no antiaircraft fire was directed at the Zero-sen before it hit the ship forward. A fire engulfed the flightdeck but was out by 0751 hrs. Although the aircraft's bomb penetrated to the hangar deck where aircraft were being armed, no fire was started.

Within seconds, a second Zero-sen dove on the escort carrier USS *Suwannee* (CVE-27). The fighter was hit by antiaircraft fire, changed its target and was then hit by a 5in. round that caused it to splash harmlessly into the sea. A third Zero-sen dove on the escort carrier USS *Petrof Bay* (CVE-80), but was also hit by antiaircraft fire and missed. The final aircraft to attack initially selected *Petrof Bay* too, but it ended up striking *Suwannee*'s flightdeck forward of the aft elevator after being damaged in its initial dive. This time, the Zero-sen's 551lb bomb penetrated to the main deck, but the hole in the flightdeck was quickly repaired and flight operations resumed some two hours after the attack. For the loss of six aircraft, the Japanese had placed one escort carrier out of action for more than three months and inflicted minor damage to another.

Worse was to follow for the Americans. Having just survived a surface attack by the IJN, "Taffy 3" now faced an even greater threat posed by six kamikazes and three escorts, all Zero-sens. The Japanese aircraft approached at low level before ascending to attack altitude just a few miles away, at which point they were detected by radar. With no time available for the CAP to make an interception, the first three Zero-sens dove on the escort carrier USS *Kalinin Bay* (CVE-68). The first aircraft was hit by antiaircraft fire, but its pilot remained in control. The fighter hit the flightdeck at a shallow angle and skidded overboard. The resulting fire was rapidly extinguished. The second Zero-sen to attack also hit the ship, but struck aft on the port side and caused little damage. The third aircraft missed.

The next Zero-sen to attack (at 1049 hrs) selected the escort carrier USS *Kitkun Bay* (CVE-71), the pilot aiming at the bridge but passing over the ship's small island and hitting the portside catwalk before crashing into the sea. Damage was slight.

"Taffy 3" was not done yet. Two more Zero-sens approached the escort carrier USS *White Plains* (CVE-66) with the intention of crashing into it. The first turned away

USS *St. Lo* (CVE-63) is seen from USS *Kitkin Bay* (CVE-71) shortly after it was hit by a Zero-sen on October 25, 1944. The pilot that targeted *St. Lo* conducted a skilful attack, approaching over the stern. He dropped his bomb before the aircraft hit amidships and skidded off the flightdeck. The bomb penetrated to the hangar and caused fires and explosions there, as shown in this view. Less than 30 minutes after being hit, the carrier rolled over and sank with the loss of 114 crew. *St. Lo* was the first ship to be sunk by kamikazes. (NARA)

under antiaircraft fire and the second approached from astern and missed, hitting the water close aboard the portside. The aircraft's bomb exploded when it hit the water, creating shock damage. The final kamikaze originally selected *White Plains*, but was forced to shift to the escort carrier USS *St. Lo* (CVE-63) by the heavy antiaircraft fire. The Zero-sen approached from astern as if it intended to land on the carrier, dropped its bomb, which hit the flightdeck aft, and then dove into the flightdeck amidships at a shallow angle. The aircraft skidded off the bow, but not before its fuel started a fire on the flightdeck. This was extinguished within minutes, but the bomb penetrated the flightdeck and exploded in the hangar deck where six aircraft were being fueled and armed. This caused a series of explosions, some massive enough to force the ship to be abandoned. Thirty minutes after being struck, the ship sank when fires reached its magazines.

The results of these first attacks were a resounding success, with a handful of suicide aircraft having sunk one escort carrier and damaged five more, some of which were forced to leave the fleet for repair.

KAMIKAZES UNLEASHED

The initial success on October 25 could not be immediately exploited by the Japanese. The number of aircraft and pilots available in the Philippines was limited and additional suicide units had to be organized. Finding volunteers was not an issue, and since they were veterans, training was not required. What followed was a continuing low level of attacks for the next few days until a much larger offensive could be organized. Initially, the officers of the Second Air Fleet were reluctant to commit their pilots to suicide attacks. After the demonstration of their power on October 25 and 26, these officers reversed course and began to organize kamikaze units.

On October 26, the remaining pilots of the initial kamikaze unit were thrown into battle. The first group of three aircraft (two kamikazes) vanished without a trace, but the second group of three kamikazes and two escorts found "Taffy 1". All three kamikazes penetrated the CAP and the first was spotted at about 1230 hrs attacking *Suwannee*, which had returned to operations after the damage it had suffered the previous day. The Zero-sen struck the carrier's flightdeck and skidded into a group of ten aircraft parked near the bow. Flames soon engulfed all of the aircraft and spread down into the hangar deck, where another ten aircraft had been fueled and were ready to be brought up to the flightdeck for launch. The fire in the hangar deck was quickly contained, but the flightdeck blaze raged for another two hours. When it was over 85 crewmen were dead, 58 missing and 102 wounded. USS *Sangamon* (CVE-26) and *Petrof Bay* reported near misses by the other kamikazes.

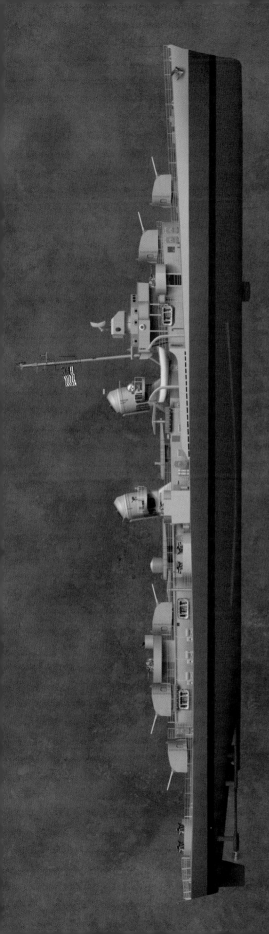

FLETCHER-CLASS DESTROYER

These artworks show a Fletcher-class destroyer in a typical 1944 configuration. Note the powerful antiaircraft battery of five 5in./38 single guns and an array of 20mm and 40mm mounts. The US Navy commissioned 175 Fletcher-class destroyers between 1942 and 1944 and 19 were lost during World War II. Twelve of these were sunk by kamikazes, with six more being so badly damaged that they were not repaired. Nine Fletcher-class destroyers were severely damaged by kamikazes during the Okinawa campaign.

Members of the Marine Detachment on board *Enterprise* shield their eyes from the sun as they scan the skies for kamikaze aircraft on October 30, 1944. Fellow TG 38.4 carriers USS *Franklin* (CV-13), left, and USS *Belleau Wood* (CVL-24) are burning furiously behind them, having already been struck by suicide attackers. *Franklin* was out of action until March 1945 and suffered 56 dead and 60 wounded, while *Belleau Wood* recorded 92 dead and 97 wounded. The light carrier did not return to action until February 1945. (NARA)

On October 29 the Japanese had enough kamikazes available to mount the largest attack to date. This operation was directed at Task Group (TG) 38.2, one of the carrier groups of TF 38. Unlike the escort carriers, the fleet carriers had a much larger aircraft complement that could generate a more effective CAP. They also possessed much more powerful screening forces. Following strikes by TG 38.2 against Japanese airfields in the Manila area, 13 kamikazes were sent to attack the carriers. The CAP took out all but one of the kamikazes. The final aircraft, a "Val", selected USS *Intrepid* (CV-11) for attack. The aircraft was engaged by 40mm and 20mm guns, but shedding parts as it approached the carrier, it flew over the flightdeck and hit the portside gun gallery. Although damage was superficial, ten sailors were killed and six wounded.

The following day TG 38.4 came under attack from six kamikazes and five escorts from Cebu. This time, five of the six suicide attackers evaded the CAP and lined up for attacks. The first targeted the new carrier USS *Franklin* (CV-13) and was able to crash into the ship's flightdeck aft. The aircraft penetrated to the hangar deck, where its bomb exploded. *Franklin* was placed out of action with a large hole in its flightdeck and the aft elevator knocked out. The second kamikaze also appeared to target *Franklin*, but after dropping a bomb that missed the large carrier, the Zero-sen pilot turned towards the light carrier USS *Belleau Wood* (CVL-24). The kamikaze struck just abaft the aft elevator, where it started a fire that spread to the 11 aircraft spotted aft. The other kamikazes did not succeed in finding a target, but the attack was still devastating. *Franklin* was out of action until March 1945 and suffered 56 dead and 60 wounded, while *Belleau Wood* recorded 92 dead and 97 wounded. The light carrier did not return to the fleet until February 1945.

An even larger onslaught was planned for November 1. TF 38 had retired to Ulithi atoll (the main US Navy operating base in the Western Pacific), in the Caroline Islands, for replenishment and a short rest, leaving the Seventh Fleet operating off Leyte to bear the brunt of the kamikazes. The Japanese targeted TG 77.1, which was comprised of three old battleships, four cruisers (one heavy and three light) and eight destroyers.

The rear-most destroyer in the formation, USS *Claxton* (DD-571), was damaged first when a "Val" just missed the ship's starboard quarter, the explosion of the aircraft's bomb creating a large hole aft. Another "Val" hit the destroyer USS *Ammen* (DD-527) amidships at a low angle and bounced off the superstructure into the water. The destroyer USS *Killen* (DD-593) was also struck by a "Val" forward, the ship suffering further damage when the aircraft's bomb scored a near miss. Finally, the destroyer USS *Abner Read* (DD-526) was struck in the aft superstructure by a "Val", starting a large fire. The aircraft's bomb had been released beforehand, and it hit the ship in the aft boiler room. The fires were never brought under control, and within 33 minutes of being struck the destroyer rolled over onto its side to become the second ship lost to a kamikaze attack.

The return of Halsey's carriers and a series of air strikes flown from these ships against Japanese airfields throughout the Philippines on November 5 and 6 suppressed the kamikaze threat for a week. The Japanese, however, were able to mount a small attack against TF 38 on November 5 when four Zero-sens attacked the carrier USS *Lexington* (CV-16). Three were shot down by antiaircraft fire, but one kamikaze hit the aft end of the island and started a large fire. Although damage was light and did not stop flight operations, 50 sailors were killed and 132 wounded.

On November 12 kamikazes returned to Leyte Gulf and struck a landing craft repair ship and five merchant ships. The latter proved hard to sink unless they were carrying munitions, although personnel casualties were heavy with more than 260 killed and almost 200 wounded. Five days later an attack transport was struck in Leyte Gulf by a kamikaze, but it suffered little damage. A merchant ship was hit on November 18.

November 25 featured another series of kamikaze attacks against two of TF 38's task groups, with USS *Hancock* (CV-19) suffering a near miss and *Intrepid* being struck by a Zero-sen. The aircraft penetrated the flightdeck before its bomb exploded, starting a fire on both the flightdeck and hangar deck. Minutes later, two more Zero-sens were spotted approaching the ship. One was taken down by antiaircraft fire, but the second did a wing over maneuver to hit the flightdeck amidships. The aircraft's bomb penetrated to the hangar deck and the resulting fires took more than two hours to extinguish. These hits forced *Intrepid* to retire to the United States for repairs, and it would not return until mid-March 1945. The light carrier USS *Cabot* (CVL-28) was also struck by a suicide aircraft that punched small holes in the flightdeck and inflicted heavy casualties on the crews in the gun gallery. Another kamikaze just missed, but the explosion of the aircraft's bomb created hull damage that forced the ship to retire to Ulithi for repairs.

TG 38.3 also suffered when two kamikazes broke through the CAP and selected USS *Essex* (CV-9) for attack. One was shot down by antiaircraft fire but the other, a "Judy", hit the flightdeck forward and started a fire after exploding in an impressive fireball. Fortunately, the damage sustained was not as bad as had been inflicted on other ships during these attacks, and CV-9 was repaired and back in action in little more than two weeks.

TF 38 experienced a very bad day on November 25, 1944. The second fleet carrier hit on that date was *Essex*, as shown here – the "Judy" struck forward on the ship's port side. Despite the large explosion, *Essex* suffered little structural damage and the ship was quickly repaired at Ulithi. (NARA)

VICE ADMIRAL TAKIJIRO ONISHI

Onishi is generally credited with being the father of kamikaze operations, being a long-time aviator and advocate of naval aviation. His early war career included a role in planning the Pearl Harbor attack and command of the naval air forces on Taiwan, which supported the invasion of the Philippines in 1941. In 1944, he was the head of the Aviation Department of the Ministry of Munitions. After the Battle of the Philippine Sea, Onishi was ordered to take over the First Air Fleet (on October 2) and defeat the expected American invasion of the Philippines.

Before leaving for his new assignment, he had informed the Chief of the Naval General Staff and the Navy Minister of his intention to form "special attack" units to target the American invasion force. Although this was not worded in such a way to explicitly state he was forming suicide units, the meaning of his intent was clear. Onishi was advised only to make sure all the pilots were volunteers.

Onishi arrived in the Philippines on October 17, just as American forces were making preliminary landings near Leyte. Upon reaching Mabalacat two days later, he found that his air fleet possessed only 100 aircraft. The size of this meager force convinced Onishi that suicide tactics were his only chance for success. On October 20 he spoke to the pilots who had volunteered for special attack missions:

> Japan is in grave danger. The salvation of our country is now beyond the power of the ministers of the state, the General Staff and lowly commanders like myself. It can come only from spirited young men such as you. Thus, on behalf of your hundred million countrymen, I ask of you this sacrifice and pray for your success.
> You are already gods, without earthly desires. But one thing you want to know is that your own crash-dive is not in vain. Regrettably, we will not be able to tell you the results. But I shall watch your efforts to the end and report your deeds to the Throne. You may all rest assured on this point.
> I ask you all to do your best.

The die was cast for a campaign of suicide attacks. Onishi was ordered to leave the Philippines on January 10, 1945 and relocate his headquarters back to Formosa. He continued in command of the First Air Fleet until May

when he was ordered to return to Japan to take the position of Vice Chief of the Naval General Staff. Even at this point of the war Onishi continued to advocate for a bitter fight to the end despite the seemingly inevitable American invasion that would lay waste to Japan.

Having ordered so many young men to their deaths, Onishi elected to take his own life after the announcement from the Emperor that Japan would surrender. On August 16, 1945 he committed ritual suicide (*seppuku*, or *hara-kiri*), but botched the attempt. He died a painful death over the period of 15 hours from his wounds since he would not allow others to hasten his ritual death.

The individual seen as the father of kamikaze attacks was Vice Admiral Takijiro Onishi, commander of the First Air Fleet in the Philippines in October 1944. His resolve to begin suicide attacks was the culmination of a year's worth of theoretical discussions among the IJN's leadership on how to overcome Japan's growing inferiority against the US Navy. (via Henry Sakaida)

COMMANDER JOHN "JIMMIE" THACH

"Jimmie" Thach was the consummate naval aviator. He began the war as commander of VF-3 and fought at the Battle of Midway. He was the originator of the "Thach Weave," which was developed to allow the standard US Navy fighter of the day, the relatively unmaneuverable F4F Wildcat, to counter the faster and more agile Zero-sen fighter. Having gained invaluable combat experience, he spent the middle part of the war on training duty.

Returning to the war, Thach was posted as the Operations Officer for Vice Admiral John S. McCain, Sr., who took command of TF 38 on October 30, 1944. In this capacity, Thach was intimately involved in trying to design methods to defeat the kamikaze threat. He came up with the so-called "Big Blue Blanket" scheme (given its name by the overall Glossy Sea Blue paint that adorned US Navy fighters) to maximize the effectiveness of the CAP. The latter was to be larger, round-the-clock and mounted at increased distances from the carriers. The key element was to place a 24-hour CAP over key Japanese airfields. This was tried as early as the Mindoro operation in late 1944, but results were mixed. It was tried again during the later part of the Okinawa campaign over airfields in southern Japan.

The use of picket destroyers was also part of Thach's concept. These were placed some 60 nautical miles from the carriers to provide extra warning of the approach of

Japanese aircraft and to "delouse" enemy machines that were following friendly aircraft back to the carriers. For the invasion of Japan, the use of picket destroyers was reduced after their vulnerability was revealed at Okinawa. In their place, the use of air- and land-based radar was envisioned.

Thach also proposed that Essex-class carriers double their fighter complement by reducing the number of Helldiver dive-bombers in an air group. The fighter complement went from a typical 38 fighters to as many as 73. The fighter aircraft were also fitted with bomb racks and rocket rails to allow them to act as fighter-bombers, allowing them to strike kamikaze bases while still maintaining the ability to fly CAP missions.

Following the war, Thach went on to even greater accomplishments. He commanded the escort carrier USS *Sicily* (CVE-118) during the Korean War, followed by Midway-class carrier USS *Franklin D. Roosevelt* (CVA-42) prior to being promoted to admiral in 1955. After holding several more key postings, Thach retired from the US Navy in 1967 as a full admiral and died in 1981.

Capt "Jimmie" Thach, pictured here in the center of the photograph, onboard the carrier USS *Shangri-La* (CV-38) with Assistant Secretary of the Navy for Air, John Sullivan, on the right, and the commander of TF 38, Vice Admiral John S. McCain, Sr., on the left. As TF 38 Operations Officer, Thach's primary concern was finding ways to defeat the kamikaze menace, which proved to be impossible using the technology of the day. (NARA)

This was the impact point of the Zero-sen that hit *Intrepid* on November 25, 1944. The damage was light and the fires started on the flightdeck were put out in ten minutes. One advantage to the lightly built flightdecks on US Navy carriers was they could be repaired relatively quickly. (NARA)

The Japanese could be satisfied with the results of their attacks on TF 38. *Intrepid, Franklin* and the light carrier *Belleau Wood* had been forced to return to the United States, while *Essex* and *Cabot* had retired to Ulithi for repairs. The first month of kamikaze attacks had brought a whole new reality to US Navy operations. The surface threat from the IJN had all but been neutralized, as had its carrier force, but the kamikaze threat was proving much more deadly than any previous conventional form of attack. The escort carriers had been savaged and even the formidable TF 38 had suffered heavily at the hands of a few kamikazes. Furthermore, efforts by TF 38 to attack Japanese airfields in the Philippines had only provided the fleet with short periods of relief. To survive against the growing kamikaze threat, US Navy defensive tactics would have to be refined and improved.

THE STORM INCREASES

The land battle on Leyte Island continued, so the ships of the Seventh Fleet were required to linger off the island in support. On November 27 the heavy ships of TG 77.2 came under attack in Leyte Gulf, with the light cruiser USS *St. Louis* (CL-49) receiving the most attention when ten kamikazes selected it for attack. At 1138 hrs an aircraft approached from astern and crashed onto the cruiser's fantail where its aviation hangar was located, starting a large fire. Five more aircraft missed the light cruiser, one by only a few feet forward. The explosion of the aircraft and its bomb damaged the hull and created enough flooding to cause *St. Louis* to list to port. The final cost was 15 dead and 21 wounded, and the light cruiser was forced back to the United States for repairs that lasted until March 1945.

Two kamikazes also selected the battleship USS *Colorado* (BB-45) for attack, one missing. The second aircraft hit one of the ship's 5in. casemate guns, killing 19 and wounding 72. *Colorado* was able to continue with its mission, however.

The Japanese returned to Leyte Gulf on November 29, but this time it was the turn of the JAAF. The first of a series of attacks was conducted by a single Ki-43 "Oscar" fighter against TG 77.2's flagship, the battleship USS *Maryland* (BB-46). The aircraft survived heavy fire to crash into the battleship between its two forward 16in. turrets. Damage was fairly light against such a heavily armored ship, but 31 sailors were killed and another 30 wounded.

Two destroyers on picket duty in Surigao Strait were much easier targets, since they were isolated from the main formation. USS *Aulick* (DD-569) spotted six kamikazes and was near-missed by two, one exploding close enough to cause devastating personnel casualties (31 dead and 64 wounded) among the exposed gun crews. USS *Saufley* (DD-465) was attacked by three kamikazes, but the destroyer was lucky since one scored only a near miss, another a glancing blow, and the last missed. *Aulick* was forced to return to the United States for repairs.

By early December the Leyte campaign was coming to a conclusion following the American landing on the western side of the island that cut the Japanese garrison off from re-supply. On December 5 kamikazes sank a landing ship medium and damaged two destroyers.

Two days later, the US Navy sent a force into Ormoc Bay to land just south of Ormoc, the major port on the western side of Leyte. The Japanese responded with heavy air attacks, both conventional and suicide. The destroyer USS *Mahan* (DD-364) and the fast transport USS *Ward* (APD-16) were assigned to patrol to the west of the landing area and came under heavy attack. The veteran *Ward*, the ship that had opened the Pacific War by firing on a Japanese midget submarine in the channel leading up to Pearl Harbor during the early morning hours of December 7, 1941, was struck by a "Betty" bomber near the waterline. The force of the large bomber crashing into the old converted destroyer made one of the aircraft's engines exit through the other side of the ship. The resulting huge fires could not be controlled and *Ward* was abandoned. Remarkably, only a single crewman was wounded. *Mahan* was attacked by at least nine aircraft and hit by three. Its captain made the decision that the resulting fires could not be controlled and the destroyer was abandoned and scuttled. Several other ships were damaged, making this day the deadliest to date.

The American beachhead at Ormoc provided kamikazes with a constant supply of targets that were relatively poorly defended. On December 11 a convoy of 13 amphibious craft and six destroyers was spotted heading to Ormoc Bay by Japanese aircraft. The CAP was only four fighters, which could not cope with the 12 kamikazes that targeted the convoy. These overwhelmed the destroyer USS *Reid* (DD-369), four kamikazes hitting the ship in quick succession and a bomb carried by one of them exploding at the ship's waterline. Within two minutes *Reid* had sunk with the loss of 103 crewmen.

MINDORO

The ultimate American objective of the Philippine campaign was Luzon. MacArthur scheduled a supporting landing on Mindoro on December 15, and as the invasion force approached its objective the ships endured a small-scale kamikaze attack on December 13. A single "Val" approached the light cruiser USS *Nashville* (CL-43) from dead astern and then targeted the ship's bridge. The resulting fire killed 133 and wounded 190 and the light cruiser was forced out of the fight. Later in the day a flight of ten aircraft (only three kamikazes) attacked the main covering force. Just one aircraft survived the CAP to dive on the destroyer USS *Haraden* (DD-585), the kamikaze exploding when it hit the forward funnel after clipping the superstructure. The ship's

A Type 99 Assault Aeroplane ("Sonia") from the Army Sekicho-Tai Special Attack Unit takes off from Bacalod, on the island of Negros, for a kamikaze mission during December 1944. (via Edward M. Young)

LST-472 was one of two tank landing ships (LSTs) sunk off Mindoro on December 15, 1944. Amphibious ships were relatively rare targets for kamikaze pilots. (NARA)

stack was blown away and 14 sailors were killed and 24 wounded. *Haraden* was forced to depart the combat area for repairs.

The landing on December 15 prompted a much larger response of five waves of kamikazes. For once the suicide aircraft focused on the transports and not their escorts, hitting two tank landing ships (LST) – *LST-472* and *LST-738* were subsequently scuttled. On December 21, a re-supply convoy headed to Mindoro was attacked with the loss of *LST-460* and *LST-749* and damage to a merchant ship. Another re-supply convoy was attacked as it left Leyte Gulf on December 28, Zero-sens crashing into two ships. The Liberty ship *John Burke* was loaded with ammunition and exploded, leaving no trace of either it or the 68 sailors onboard. The other ship survived a crash into its bridge. When the convoy arrived at Mindoro on December 30, it was subjected to a further attack. Although small in scale (only five "Vals"), it was deadly. A patrol torpedo boat tender was knocked out of the war with the loss of 59 dead and 106 wounded, the auxiliary tanker *Porcupine* was bombed and later scuttled, the destroyer USS *Gansevoort* (DD-608) was also knocked out of the war and the destroyer USS *Pringle* (DD-477) was slightly damaged.

The final attack of the Mindoro operation was recorded on January 4, 1945 when a single kamikaze hit the merchantman *Lewis L. Dyche*, which was carrying ammunition. For the second time in a week a ship vaporized, along with its crew of 71 men.

PHILIPPINES FINALE

The climax of the Philippines campaign was the American invasion of Luzon. Knowing that the loss of Luzon meant the loss of the Philippines, the Japanese mounted ten consecutive days of kamikaze attacks on the invasion force.

The ordeal began on January 4 as the invasion fleet made its way through the Sulu Sea en route to Luzon. Despite 18 escort carriers being assigned to provide CAP, a single IJNAF twin-engined P1Y Ginga (known as "Frances" to the Allies) bomber evaded radar detection and was not spotted until it was diving on the escort carrier USS *Ommaney Bay* (CVE-79). With complete surprise, the bomber hit the ship's island and then the flightdeck before smashing into the sea. This caused little damage, but the aircraft's two bombs had penetrated through to the forward hangar deck and engine room before they exploded. All power was soon lost, which made it impossible to fight the fires in the hangar deck that were being fed by refueled and rearmed aircraft. *Ommaney Bay* was abandoned an hour after the suicide hit and was later scuttled.

The attacks on January 5 were more severe. The first two waves of kamikazes were defeated by the CAP, but the third of 16 kamikazes and four escorts broke through in the late afternoon. The first group hit the No. 2 turret of the heavy cruiser USS *Louisville*

ENGAGING THE ENEMY

This kamikaze pilot flying his Zero-sen fighter has put himself in a perfect position to strike a serious blow against the US Navy. The target below him is an Essex-class carrier, whose crew has been late in spotting the suicide aircraft making a diving attack – the IJNAF pilot may have used cloud cover to mask his approach, or closed on the carrier at wave-top height before pulling up into a steep climb and then bunting over in to his death dive.

The ship's myriad gunners have begun to engage the Zero-sen with 20mm and 40mm antiaircraft fire, as well as a handful of 5in. rounds, but at this late stage in the attack

it is very doubtful that this will stop the kamikaze from striking the ship. Indeed, if the Zero-sen pilot does not flinch at the last moment, he will hit the ship. If skillful enough, he will release his 551lb bomb before striking the carrier as close to the rear aircraft elevator as possible – one of the vulnerable spots he had been trained to hit. Given the large number of aircraft spotted on the flightdeck, all of which are probably fully fueled and armed ready for their next launch cycle, this carrier is about to receive serious damage that could threaten the ship itself.

(CA-28) and the Royal Australian Navy (RAN) destroyer HMAS *Arunta*. The RAN heavy cruiser HMAS *Australia* was also hit and the escort carriers came under heavy attack. Two Zero-sens selected USS *Manila Bay* (CVE-61) for treatment, the first hitting the flightdeck in the area of the island and penetrating through to the hangar deck, but the resulting fire was quickly brought under control. USS *Savo Island* (CVE-78) suffered a near miss and three of the four Zero-sens that targeted USS *Tulagi* (CVE-72) were shot down by antiaircraft fire. The fourth hit the destroyer escort USS *Stafford* (DE-411) and created a large hole that flooded the engine room. The ship was forced to return to the United States for repairs.

Even more carnage was in store for January 6. Thirteen ships were hit, although all but one survived. The only ship to be sunk was the destroyer-minesweeper USS *Long* (DMS-12), which was attacked by two Zero-sens. USS *Brooks* (APD-10) – another converted old four-stacker destroyer now being used as a high speed transport and minesweeper – was hit in the portside, starting a fire amidships. Although the latter was eventually contained, the 25-year-old ship had to be towed back to the California, where it was declared a total constructive loss.

Five other destroyers and a destroyer-minesweeper were damaged that same day, as were several heavy ships. The battleships USS *New Mexico* (BB-40) and USS *California* (BB-44) were both hit by single kamikazes, although their armor prevented crippling damage. Nevertheless, the latter suffered 44 killed and 155 wounded, although both ships remained on station. The light cruiser USS *Columbia* (CL-56) was hit twice, while the heavy cruiser USS *Minneapolis* (CA-36) suffered light damage. *Louisville* was hit again and this time forced to leave the battle area for repairs, while *Australia*, quickly becoming a suicide magnet, was also hit for the second time. This level of damage was unsustainable, as was the tally of 167 sailors dead and more than 500 wounded. The escort carriers had been incapable of providing adequate air cover, with CAP operations being hindered by nearby land features that interfered with ship-borne radar.

Allied sailors enjoyed a brief respite on January 7 when no successful attacks were recorded, although the kamikazes returned with a vengeance on the 8th when primarily JAAF aircraft attacked the invasion fleet. An LST and an attack transport were damaged and *Australia* was hit for the third time. The escort carriers came in for the worst treatment, however, with an "Oscar" from a large group of some 20 aircraft hitting USS *Kadashan Bay* (CVE-76) at its waterline, creating a large hole. Although the aircraft's bombs did not explode, the carrier was nevertheless out of action until mid-April. Later in the day a group of six kamikazes went after *Kitkun Bay*. Four of the aircraft were shot down by the CAP, but an "Oscar" crashed into the ship at the waterline amidships on the portside. This caused extensive flooding and a loss of power, although the ship was eventually saved. It too was forced out of action for months, having had 16 sailors killed and 37 wounded.

By now the Japanese were simply running out of aircraft and the flow of aerial reinforcements to the Philippines had been stopped. Nevertheless, the Allied fleet was subjected to five more days of spasmodic attacks. On January 9 two destroyer escorts were hit and the light cruiser *Columbia* struck for the third time. On this occasion the damage inflicted was more severe and the ship was ordered to leave the battle area with another 24 crew dead and 68 wounded. *Australia* was also hit again and forced to seek repairs. Finally, two "Vals" selected the veteran battleship USS *Mississippi* (BB-41) for attack. One struck a glancing blow from the ship's forward superstructure down to the hull, and although the structural damage that resulted was light, 23 sailors were killed and 63 wounded.

A destroyer escort was hit on January 10 and a JAAF Ki-45 "Nick" struck an attack transport loaded with troops – 32 were killed and 157 wounded. The next day another "Nick" flew into a fast transport, causing serious damage as well as killing 38 and wounding 49. On January 12 an LST and two destroyer escorts were damaged. Merchant ships also came under attack, with three suffering hits – aboard

Jim Laurier

one ship, 129 US Army troops were killed. The final attacks of the campaign were recorded on January 13 when a JAAF Ki-84 "Frank" fighter crashed into the escort carrier USS *Salamaua* (CVE-96). One of the aircraft's bombs exploded in the hangar deck and the second passed through the ship, creating a hole near the waterline. The aircraft carrier was temporarily left with no power and major fires, the latter killing 15 sailors and wounding a further 88. Although damage control was successful, the ship was out of the war until April. Also on this day an LST and a troop transport were hit.

The effectiveness of the Philippines attacks had clearly diminished after the Japanese ran out of experienced pilots. Novice aviators may have possessed the same fervor to crash into American ships, but they did not always possess the skill required to fly their aircraft, often damaged, to hit a maneuvering target. Aiding their cause, however, was the presence of land near the ships, as this often confused American radar. Furthermore, land-based American air power was slow to be introduced, placing the burden on the escort carriers, which failed to provide a strong continuous CAP. Overall, American anti-kamikaze tactics were still immature.

PRELUDE TO OKINAWA

Following the end of the Luzon invasion and until the beginning of the invasion of Okinawa on April 1, there was a relative lull in kamikaze activity. On February 10 leadership of the kamikaze effort was given to Vice Admiral Matome Ugaki when he assumed command of the Fifth Air Fleet based in southern Japan. It was this unit that would conduct most of the IJNAF's kamikaze operations for the rest of the war.

Even during this interlude, the Japanese still found opportunities to strike US Navy forces. On January 21 two small waves of kamikazes, with a total of only nine aircraft, found TF 38 off Formosa. A Zero-sen from the first wave penetrated all defenses and crashed into the carrier USS *Ticonderoga* (CV-14), which had its air group fully fueled and armed on deck for a strike. The enemy fighter hit aft of the forward elevator and its bomb exploded, starting an intense fire among the aircraft on the hangar deck. An aircraft from the second wave then hit the island. The carrier survived, but at a cost of 143 sailors killed and missing and another 202 wounded. *Ticonderoga* was out of the war until May.

On February 19 the US Marines Corps landed on Iwo Jima. The invasion fleet was tethered to the island, making it easy for the kamikazes to find a target. The Japanese response waited until February 21, when a group of 32 aircraft, including 20 kamikazes, was sent to attack the carriers protecting the invasion fleet. The strike was supported by aircraft dropping chaff to confuse American radar operators. The first six kamikazes came out of low clouds to attack the old fleet carrier USS *Saratoga* (CV-3). Of these, five hit or near-missed the ship. An additional kamikaze struck the ship from a second wave, but in spite of this cumulative damage, the carrier was never in any danger of sinking and the crew successfully extinguished all fires. The cost of this attack was 123 dead and 192 wounded and another carrier forced to return to the United States for repairs.

Radar performance that evening was not good, and another group penetrated the CAP to select the escort carrier USS *Bismarck Sea* (CVE-95) for attack. A "Betty" twin-engined bomber came in low, survived hits from the ship's antiaircraft guns and crashed into the carrier abeam the aft aircraft elevator. A fire broke out among the aircraft packed into the hangar bay, and within minutes an additional explosion, possibly caused by a second kamikaze, made further firefighting operations impossible, dooming the ship. *Bismarck Sea* sank, taking 119 members of its crew with it.

Another spectacular kamikaze attack was conducted on the Fast Carrier Task Force as it lay in Ulithi Atoll, which was the main US Navy operating base in the Western Pacific. On March 9 a Japanese reconnaissance aircraft flying from Truk Atoll spotted the fast carriers at anchor. Despite the fact that Ulithi was more than 800 nautical miles from the home islands, the Japanese determined that "Frances" bombers could reach the target, primarily because the mission was going to be one way only.

The tremendous distance did cause problems, and the complex operation fell apart soon after being launched at dusk on March 11. Of the 24 "Frances" bombers making up the attack force, 11 returned due to mechanical issues. Poor weather and navigation meant the remaining 13 bombers did not find Ulithi as expected, and all but two either landed on a Japanese-held island or fell into the ocean because of fuel exhaustion.

Vice Admiral Matome Ugaki, commander of the Fifth Air Fleet, took charge of *Kikusui* operations, which ran from April 6 to June 22, 1945. Following the announcement of Emperor Hirohito's surrender, and to atone for the many deaths under his command, Ugaki stripped his uniform of its gold braid and took off from Oita airfield with a flight of "Judy" dive-bombers on the afternoon of August 15. A radio transmission was heard, which said that he was diving on an enemy ship. The following day, Ugaki's aircraft and body were discovered on a sandbar at Iheya Jima, 20 miles northwest of the northern tip of Okinawa. (via Henry Sakaida)

Although the anchorage was entirely lit, one bomber crashed into a lighted baseball field on a nearby island. The second hit the new fleet carrier USS *Randolph* (CV-15) in its fantail, the kamikaze's bomb exploding and creating a hole in the flightdeck. Fortunately, the lack of fuel onboard the aircraft parked on the flightdeck prevented the ship from catching fire. Repairs were completed locally within a month.

Following the bold attack on Ulithi, TF 58 sortied to attack southern Japan to reduce the threat to the Okinawa invasion, planned for April 1. On March 18 TF 58 hit kamikaze bases on Kyushu. In response Ugaki's airmen mounted conventional and kamikaze attacks. One "Frances" crashed close to kamikaze-magnet *Intrepid* and sprayed the carrier with debris and flaming fuel. This created a brief hangar fire, but the ship remained in action. The following day, a bomb from a kamikaze hit *Wasp* (CV-18) and caused a significant fire and casualties that totaled 101 dead and 269 wounded. The ship was able to remain in action, however.

SUSTAINED TERROR – KAMIKAZES AT OKINAWA

The preface to the Okinawa campaign was the American seizure of Kerama Retto, a group of small islands just west of Okinawa. This began on March 26 and prompted an immediate Japanese reaction. Limited attacks on March 26 and 27 resulted in damage to several ships, but none were sunk. On March 31 the heavy cruiser USS *Indianapolis* (CA-35), flagship of the Fifth Fleet, was struck aft by a kamikaze and forced to retire to the United States for repairs.

The landing on Okinawa on April 1 did not bring the massed kamikaze attacks that the campaign was eventually known for. Limited attacks that day damaged an LST, two attack transports, a destroyer-minelayer and the battleship USS *West Virginia* (BB-48). Aside from the LST, all ships eventually returned to service. On April 2, the Japanese caught a lightly defended troop convoy near Kerama Retto and hit three

The battleship USS *Nevada* (BB-36) was hit by a single kamikaze on March 27, 1945 while participating in the pre-invasion bombardment of Okinawa. The aircraft hit near 14in. gun Turret No. 3, but caused little damage. Nearby exposed antiaircraft gun crews suffered 11 dead and 49 wounded, however. (NARA)

transports and the fast transport USS *Dickerson* (APD-21). The aircraft that hit the latter ship was identified as a JAAF Ki-45 "Nick", *Dickerson*'s bridge being struck. Flames soon spread to the forward magazines, forcing the ship to be abandoned. It was subsequently deemed to be fit only for scrapping.

Ugaki waited until April 6 to unleash his first massed strike. This was to be the first in a series of attacks each named Floating Chrysanthemum (*Kikusui*), which had symbolic meaning attached to the Emperor. More than 200 kamikazes, plus escorts, were used in the first day's attack, which began after 1500 hrs. This was the biggest single kamikaze event of the war to date. At the end of the two-day operation, nine ships had been destroyed and another 11 damaged. Total personnel losses were also steep – 370 dead and 475 wounded.

In order to provide earlier warning of an attack on the invasion fleet, the US Navy established a number of Radar Picket (RP) stations at varying distances from the invasion area. These were manned by destroyers and a fleet of smaller craft. They quickly became favorite Japanese targets, since they believed it necessary to suppress the RPs in order to allow the main force of kamikazes to penetrate to the invasion area. On April 6 the three RPs on a direct path from Kyushu to Okinawa came under heavy attack, with the destroyer USS *Bush* (DD-529) on RP 1 being hit by two kamikazes and sunk with the loss of 87 dead and 42 wounded. The destroyer USS *Colhoun* (DD-801) on RP 2 was hit by at least four kamikazes and scuttled after midnight. A further 35 sailors lost their lives and 21 were wounded.

While kamikazes were pummeling the RPs, the bombardment force was also under attack in the waters off the island of Ie Shima. A total of four destroyers were hit and two

The veteran carrier *Enterprise* came under kamikaze attack on April 11, 1945, a "Judy" hitting the portside 40mm quad gun mounts. The real damage was inflicted by the aircraft's bomb, however, which exploded under the carrier's hull. The carrier was forced to go to the Ulithi anchorage for three weeks of repairs. (NARA)

were eventually declared total constructive losses, while the other two were repaired but did not return to service until after the war. Also in the anchorage at Ie Shima, a Zero-sen hit *LST-447*, which burned out and sank, and the Victory ships *Hobbs Victory* and *Logan Victory*, carrying ammunition, were struck too. Both were abandoned and later scuttled on April 7.

Elsewhere, the destroyer-minesweeper USS *Emmons* (DMS-22) was hit by five kamikazes in quick succession, resulting in the ship having to be scuttled with the loss of 64 dead and 71 wounded. A destroyer and a destroyer escort were also hit by a single kamikaze and subsequently declared constructive total losses. Another destroyer and destroyer-minesweeper were hit and later repaired, but not until after the war. The following day, a destroyer escort and the battleship *Maryland* were damaged. TF 58 also came under attack on April 7, with the fleet carrier *Hancock* being hit by a single kamikaze. Although damage was light, 62 sailors were killed and 71 wounded.

On April 11, 1945, the battleship USS *Missouri* (BB-63) was hit amidships by a Zero-sen on its starboard side. Here, gun crews watch the aircraft approach, which when it hit exploded in a large fireball, but caused no real damage to the heavily-armored battleship. (NARA)

In the four days between *Kikusui* Nos. 1 and 2, only limited attacks were recorded. Two more destroyers were damaged, and on April 11 TF 58 came under attack again. *Enterprise* was damaged by two "Judy" aircraft and forced to miss three weeks of service undergoing repair. The destroyer USS *Kidd* (DD-661) was also damaged, with the cost of 38 dead and 55 wounded, but it survived to serve after the war and eventually be preserved in Louisiana as a museum ship. In another demonstration that battleships were not the best kamikaze target, USS *Missouri* (BB-63) was hit below its main deck on the armored belt. Aside from scarring the warship's paint, there was no damage inflicted.

The second massed kamikaze attack took place on April 12–13, and included some 185 suicide aircraft. Again, the picket destroyers came in for special attention. RP 1 was the scene of more desperate combat as the destroyers USS *Cassin Young* (DD-793) and USS *Purdy* (DD-734), with four smaller craft, came under attack from a group of some 25 IJNAF and JAAF aircraft on the afternoon of the 12th. The two destroyers were quickly damaged and forced to head to Kerama Retto for repairs. One of the escorting craft was sunk by a hit from a "Val" and a second damaged by two direct hits and a near miss.

To reinforce RP 1, two more destroyers were sent over, and one was damaged by an Ohka rocket-powered bomb. The Ohka (Cherry Blossom) enjoyed one of its few successes when, that same day, the destroyer USS *Mannert L. Abele* (DD-733) came under attack on RP 14. The ship was hit by a Zero-sen and then finished off by an Ohka, with its large 2,646lb warhead. The destroyer sank in only four minutes after the first hit, with the loss of 79 dead and 35 wounded.

In other attacks on April 12, the destroyer-minelayer USS *Lindsey* (DM-32) was attacked by a group of seven suicide aircraft. A hit forward removed the bow back to the second 5in. mount, but the ship survived and was later repaired. A destroyer escort

USS *Lindsey* (DM-32) had its forward hull sections completely destroyed by two kamikazes on April 12, 1945. The second kamikaze hit the bow and set off the magazine for the forward 5in. mount – 57 crewmen were killed or missing and another 57 wounded. The ship was towed to safety and later repaired. (NARA)

was hit on its bridge by a single "Val" and later declared a constructive total loss. Two other destroyer escorts were also damaged, although they were repairable. An attack on the fire support group resulted in damage to a destroyer by a single B6N "Jill," the ship being hit while escorting the battleship USS *Tennessee* (BB-43). The latter was struck by a "Val" during the same attack, although the ship was able to remain on station.

Kikusui No. 3 was launched on 16–17 April, and it included 165 IJNAF and JAAF aircraft. Once again, the Japanese focused on the picket destroyers. The most epic battle fought on this occasion was the encounter between USS *Laffey* (DD-724) and at least 23 suicide aircraft. Despite being hit six times, the destroyer survived. The destroyer USS *Bryant* (DD-665), manning RP 2, was attacked by six aircraft and hit on the base of the bridge by a Zero-sen. The suicide aircraft killed 34 sailors and wounded a further 33.

On RP 14, *Pringle* suffered the worst when three "Vals" selected it for attack. The first was destroyed by 5in. gunfire, but the second conducted a steep dive and hit the

USS *Laffey* (DD-724), an Allen M. Sumner-class destroyer, was a salient example of the determination of the US Navy's warship crews to fight back against kamikaze attack. Hit by six kamikazes and three bombs, the destroyer survived intensive attacks on April 16, 1945. This photograph shows the damage sustained by the ship, including a destroyed rear 5in./38 turret, which was hit by a "Val". Its bomb ignited the turret's powder magazine, destroying the gun mount and starting a major fire. Shortly thereafter, another "Val" crashed into the burning turret after it had been set alight by *Laffey*'s gunners. (NHHC)

ship in the mast area. The aircraft's bomb exploded in the forward fireroom with catastrophic results. Within two minutes the ship had broken in two, sinking three minutes later. The destroyer-minesweeper USS *Harding* (DMS-28) was moving to RP 14 when it was attacked, a single kamikaze crashing close aboard and its bomb exploding under the ship casing. Having suffered extensive underwater damage, *Harding* was forced to return to the United States and was subsequently declared a constructive total loss.

Only a small number of aircraft from *Kikusui* No. 3 were able to find and attack TF 58. Nevertheless, *Intrepid* was hit for the fourth time by a kamikaze, the suicide aircraft scoring a direct hit near the aft elevator and penetrating to the hangar deck, where a large fire was created. Excellent damage control saved the ship and repaired the hole in the flightdeck, but this time the carrier was forced to return to the United States for repairs. By the time these were completed the war was over.

On April 27–28 *Kikusui* No. 4 was launched, consisting of a wave of 115 suicide aircraft. The attacks began on the night of the 27th under a full moon. At 2041 hrs, a suicide aircraft struck the clearly marked and fully illuminated hospital ship USS *Comfort* (AH-6), killing 30 and wounding 48. The following day, two destroyers on RP 2 were slightly damaged, while the destroyer USS *Wadsworth* (DD-516) on

Intrepid was hit for the last time by kamikazes on April 16, 1945, the suicide aircraft striking the carrier near the aft elevator and penetrating into the hangar bay, where is started a large fire. Crewmen are shown here fighting the blaze, which was put out in under an hour. Effective damage control by US Navy personnel was critically important, and it helped to save many ships hit by kamikazes. (NARA)

On April 29, 1945 USS *Hazelwood* (DD-531) was targeted by three Zero-sen kamikazes while escorting a fast carrier group off Okinawa. Although the ship managed to maneuver out of the way of the first two A6Ms, a third dove out of cloud cover astern of the destroyer and hit the No. 2 stack before crashing into the base of the bridge. The explosion of the aircraft's bomb and flaming gasoline caused heavy casualties (46 dead, including the ship's commanding officer, and 26 wounded). Although badly damaged, *Hazelwood* was eventually repaired after the war and returned to fleet service in 1951. (via Bill Campbell)

USS *Aaron Ward* (DM-34) was laid down as an Allen M. Sumner-class destroyer and converted into a destroyer-minelayer before commissioning. The ship endured an intensive kamikaze attack on RP 10 on May 3, 1945, this photograph showing the damage inflicted on *Aaron Ward*'s aft section after it suffered five kamikaze hits or near-misses. The ship was eventually declared a constructive total loss. (NHHC)

RP 10 was attacked by 12 aircraft, but only slightly damaged. The merchant transport *Canada Victory*, carrying munitions, was struck and sank in ten minutes and a fast transport was also hit and subsequently declared a constructive total loss.

In the period before the next mass kamikaze operation, the Japanese continued small-level attacks. On April 29 a kamikaze crashed into the base of the bridge of destroyer USS *Hazelwood* (DD-531). The impact of the explosion of the aircraft's bomb caused heavy casualties (46 dead and 26 wounded), although the ship was eventually repaired. On the same day Hazelwood's sister-ship, USS *Haggard* (DD-555), was also hit, the destroyer being towed to Kerama Retto, but never repaired. Two days later the large minelayer USS *Terror* (CM-5) was struck by a suicide aircraft. Again, the personnel toll was heavy, with 48 dead and 123 wounded, but the ship survived.

On May 3–4 the Japanese launched *Kikusui* No. 5, which consisted of 125 aircraft, at the American fleet. Again, the radar picket ships came in for special attention. Shortly before dusk on the 3rd the destroyer USS *Little* (DD-803) and the destroyer-minelayer USS *Aaron Ward* (DM-34), with four support craft, were operating on RP 10 west of Kerama Retto. *Little* was attacked by four kamikazes, one hitting amidships and breaking the destroyer's back. It duly sunk just over an hour later, the ship's crew having suffered 62 fatalities and 27 wounded. The Japanese pilots then turned their attention to *Aaron Ward*. It was hit by five aircraft and suffered severe flooding aft, although the crew saved the ship and it was towed to Kerama Retto. After returning to the United States for repairs, it was declared a constructive total loss.

This dramatic photograph was taken seconds before this aircraft, probably a D4Y3 Suisei, narrowly missed the escort carrier USS *Sangamon* (CVE-26) on May 4, 1945 during *Kikusui* No. 5. (NARA)

The following day things became even worse. The destroyer USS *Luce* (DD-522), assigned to RP 12, was hit by two kamikazes that broke through the CAP. Minutes later the crew was ordered to abandon ship. Of the 335 personnel aboard, 149 were killed and 94 wounded. The destroyers USS *Morrison* (DD-560) and USS *Ingraham* (DD-444) were manning the northernmost station (RP 1) with four support craft when, from 0715 hrs, 40–50 suicide aircraft began their attacks. *Morrison* was hit by two Zero-sens and then finished off by two floatplanes carrying bombs. Of the 331 personnel aboard, only 71 were uninjured. *Ingraham* was hit on the waterline on its port side and seriously damaged.

On RP 14, the destroyer-minelayer USS *Shea* (DM-30) was damaged by kamikaze attacks that included an Ohka. Fortunately for *Shea*, the rocket-powered bomb's huge warhead exploded away from the ship. Two more destroyers were near-missed on RP 2, and a destroyer-minelayer was slightly damaged by a single kamikaze on RP 10. Other attacks during *Kikusui* No. 5 resulted in damage to both the light cruiser USS *Birmingham* (CL-62) by a single "Oscar" and to the escort carrier *Sangamon*, also by a single hit. The latter caused severe fires, and although the ship was saved, it had not been repaired by war's end.

On May 9, before the start of the next mass attack, the destroyer escorts USS *England* (DE-635) and USS *Oberrender* (DE-344) were hit and seriously damaged. Both were eventually declared constructive total losses.

LAST *KIKUSUI* OPERATIONS

Ugaki ordered five more massed attacks before the bloodletting off Okinawa came to an end. By this point the quality of Japanese pilots was demonstrably lower, thus reducing the effectiveness of the attacks. The battle for Okinawa was also decided, so

Moments later, at 1933 hrs, *Sangamon* was hit by a bomb dropped by a kamikaze, as well as parts of the aircraft itself. Both the weapon and the aircraft penetrated the flightdeck before exploding, causing extensive damage, and starting fires on the flightdeck, the fuel deck and in the hangar bay (seen here). By 2230 hrs the fires were finally under control and the ship headed to Kerama Retto so that temporary repairs could be made. Although *Sangamon* had been saved, it was not repaired post-war. (NARA)

Sangamon's flightdeck was littered with the charred remains of Avengers and Hellcats, and both of its elevators were blown out of place by explosions in the hangar bay. (NARA)

In another well-known photograph from the Pacific War, USS *Bunker Hill* (CV-17) has just been hit by two kamikazes on May 11, 1945. Four bomb-equipped Zero-sens of the Kanoya-based 7th Showa Special Attack Squadron (two of which were flown by Lt(jg) Seizo Yasunori and Ens Kiyoshi Ogawa) had found TF 58 without being detected by radar. With their approach masked by low cloud cover, the pilots used the element of surprise to attack *Bunker Hill*. The Zero-sens (and their bombs) of Yasunori and Ogawa struck the ship within 30 seconds of each other. The intense black smoke indicates that fully-fueled aircraft on the flightdeck have been set ablaze and that the crew's epic efforts to save their ship have begun. The crew eventually managed to bring the conflagration under control and save the ship, but not before more than 346 sailors had been killed, 43 listed as missing (and never found) and 264 wounded. (NARA)

the Japanese shifted into a force preservation mode in expectation of the decisive battle for the home islands.

Kikusui No. 6 commenced on May 10 and expended another 150 aircraft. Some 50 of these concentrated on the destroyers USS *Hugh W. Hadley* (DD-774) and USS *Evans* (DD-552) operating on RP 15 northwest of Ie Shima. The two ships put up an excellent defense, aided by the Japanese pilots' decision to conduct individual attacks that allowed each ship to mass its firepower on successive targets. *Hadley* claimed 12 kamikazes and *Evans* another 19. Eventually, both ships were overwhelmed and struck by multiple suicide aircraft. Although neither destroyer was sunk, they were both declared constructive total losses after being towed back to San Francisco.

The next morning, the kamikazes scored one of their biggest successes of the entire war when four bomb-equipped Zero-sens found TF 58 without being detected by radar. With their approach masked by low cloud cover, the pilots used the element of surprise to attack USS *Bunker Hill* (CV-17). Two of the Zero-sens (and their bombs) struck the ship within 30 seconds of each other, creating huge fires on the flight and hangar decks among the fully fueled and armed aircraft that were being prepared for launching. The crew eventually managed to bring the conflagration under control and save the ship, but not before more than 346 sailors had been killed, 43 listed as missing (and never found) and 264 wounded. *Bunker Hill* was sent home to be repaired, and it was still in the Bremerton Naval Shipyard when the war ended.

Between May 12 and 20 sporadic attacks continued that resulted in the destroyer USS *Thatcher* (DD-514) – hit by a Ki-43 – and the fast transport USS *Chase* (APD-54) both being declared as constructive total losses after being struck on the 20th. Six days earlier the veteran carrier *Enterprise* was hit by a single Zero-sen aft of the forward elevator and finally knocked out of the war. The battleship *New Mexico* had been struck yet again on May 12, but it had suffered little damage. Casualties to exposed personnel were high, however, including 54 dead.

Kikusui No. 7 was conducted between May 23–25 with 175 suicide aircraft, and despite the high number of aircraft committed, damage was relatively light. The fast transport USS *Barry* (APD-29) was hit on the 25th by a single kamikaze and eventually sunk the following month, as noted later in this chapter. That same day the fast transport USS *Bates* (APD-47) was damaged and later capsized. Another fast transport and a destroyer escort were also damaged and not repaired until after the war.

Kikusui No. 8 commenced on May 27 and ended two days later following the expenditure of 110 aircraft. On the first day of the new offensive the destroyer-minesweeper USS *Forrest* (DMS-24) was hit by a single kamikaze and not repaired after

Ki-9 Akatombo (Red Dragonfly/"Spruce") trainers found abandoned at Kikushi airfield, near Nagasaki, in 1945. They had been crudely prepared for suicide missions by the installation of a drum full of gasoline in the rear cockpit. The aircraft closest to the camera has been marked with a typical kamikaze emblem – the cherry blossom – on its tail, along with the Kana symbol "To" for Tokko (special attack) and the Kazekaoru inscription "Rise on a perfumed breeze, fall in a rain of cherry blossoms". Aircraft such as these proved difficult to detect on radar due to their material composition and their low-level attack profiles. They were also hard to shoot down as cannon rounds would simply pass through their wood and fabric fuselage and wings. (NARA)

the war. The destroyer USS *Braine* (DD-630) was hit by two kamikazes that same day on RP 5, but it survived and was repaired. The destroyer USS *Drexler* (DD-741) was attacked by six JAAF "Nicks" on the 28th, the ship quickly sinking with the loss of 158 crew. A further 52 were wounded. The next day the destroyer USS *Shubrick* (DD-639) was also hit by a twin-engined aircraft and eventually declared a constructive total loss.

Only 50 aircraft were committed to *Kikusui* No. 9, which was conducted from June 3 to July 7. On June 5 the battleship *Mississippi* and heavy cruiser *Louisville* were both struck, but their heavy protection allowed them to remain on-station. The following day the destroyer-minelayer USS *J. William Ditter* (DM-31) was attacked by a large number of suicide aircraft and subsequently declared a constructive total loss. On 10 June, while manning RP 15A, the destroyer USS *William D. Porter* (DD-579) was attacked by a single "Val". The aircraft missed and crashed into the sea, but its bomb exploded under the ship's hull which caused progressive flooding leading to the destroyer's loss.

The final act was left to 45 suicide aircraft of *Kikusui* No. 10 between June 21–22. These were only able to sink a single landing craft and the already crippled fast transport *Barry* and damage several other ships. *Barry* had been towed to the anchorage at Kerama Retto three days after it had been attacked on May 25, where it was found to be too extensively damaged to warrant repair or salvage. Stripped of any useful gear, the veteran warship was decommissioned on June 21. Later that same day it was towed from the harbor of Kerama Retto to be used as a decoy for kamikazes. While under tow by fleet tug USS *Lipan* (ATF-85), *Barry* was again attacked by two kamikazes and sunk, along with one of its escorts.

The final US Navy ship to go down at the hands of a kamikaze was the destroyer USS *Callaghan* (DD-792) on RP 9A on July 28, the ship being attacked by a wooden-and-fabric biplane that approached undetected at low level. The aircraft struck the destroyer on its starboard side and exploded, while one of its bombs penetrated the after engine room prior to detonating. Fires ignited antiaircraft shells, preventing other ships from coming to its aid, and the ship soon flooded. It sunk at 0235 hrs on the 28th with the loss of 47 crewmembers. With this, the war's largest and most destructive air-sea campaign was over.

STATISTICS AND ANALYSIS

The question remains, was the kamikaze campaign effective? The exact number of suicide attackers sent against Allies ships from October 1944 until the end of the war is difficult to determine with certainty. An accepted source states that 3,913 Japanese aircrew died conducting some 3,000 kamikaze missions. This included 2,525 IJNAF and 1,388 JAAF personnel. Of these 3,000 missions, only one-third got to the point where they conducted an attack on a ship. If they got to this point, they had about a 36 percent chance of success. Some 367 kamikazes hit their target or gained a near miss close enough to cause damage. In total, each kamikaze aircraft had about a 9.4 percent chance of hitting a target, and if it did, it caused an average of 40 casualties.

The cost to the US Navy and its Allies was 66 ships or craft sunk or never repaired and almost 400 damaged in some measure. Of the ships or craft that never returned to service, only 39 were sunk outright. Coming up with personnel casualties is difficult, but approximately 15,000 is generally accepted as accurate. This figure includes 6,190 killed and 8,760 wounded.

The US Navy certainly took the kamikaze threat very seriously from the opening suicide attacks. An early report from February 1945 using data from October 12 to November 30, 1944 determined that more than half of the 108 kamikaze attacks resulted in some kind of damage. The calculations indicated that 5.1 percent of targets were sunk and another 47.4 percent suffered some sort of damage. When compared to conventional attacks from the period of the Marianas campaign, the bottom line was that a kamikaze attack was seven to ten times more likely to cause damage than a conventional attack. The notion that kamikaze attacks were far more effective than

conventional attacks is confirmed by the fact that from October 1944 through to April 1945, the average number of attacking aircraft required to score a hit was 37 for conventional attack and 3.6 for kamikaze attacks.

In the Philippines campaign, the kamikaze showed itself to be a viable weapon that could have tactical effects. For the expenditure of 500–600 aircraft, the kamikazes caused some degree of damage to 140 ships and craft, of which 17 were sunk or scuttled. As already outlined, the largest ship of those sunk was an escort carrier. The others were a collection of smaller ships, including three destroyers, a fast transport, six amphibious units (most small), three other small combatants and three merchant ships. Although significant, these losses had no operational or strategic impact.

After the kamikazes' spectacular debut in the Philippines, by the time of the Okinawa campaign it was clear that their overall effectiveness was declining. This was true for two main reasons – the attacks were now being mounted by novice pilots and the US Navy was getting better at countering the threat. Illustrating this trend are the numbers of attacks from February to May 1945, when an estimated 1,100 kamikaze sorties were flown. Of these, roughly 500 were accounted for by the fighter CAP and 420 were shot down by antiaircraft fire and scored no hit. This left about 180 that hit a target. The bottom line was that by 1945, 84 percent of kamikazes were missing their target.

In 1945, the number of sunk and damaged ships went up dramatically, but this was a function of the much larger numbers of aircraft being used as kamikazes. A total of 32 ships were sunk, including two escort carriers, 13 destroyers or destroyer-like ships, three fast transports and nine other amphibious ships, one small combatant and four merchant ships. Additionally, many damaged ships were not deemed worth repairing at war's end. It is clear that such totals were not going to turn the Pacific War in Japan's favor.

Despite the fact that kamikazes were dealing real blows to the US Navy, an obvious side effect was that these operations were also causing huge losses to the Japanese.

This close-up photograph of the stern section of USS *Leutze* (DD-481) at anchor off Kerama Retto on April 9, 1945 reveals the extent of the damage the ship had suffered three days earlier in a kamikaze attack. The destroyer was alongside the burning USS *Newcomb* (DD-586), assisting its crew tackling fires started by three kamikaze hits, when a fourth aircraft hit the destroyer and skidded across its deck into *Leutze*. Its bomb then detonated against *Leutze*'s port quarter, inflicting the damage seen here. Recalling its firefighting parties from *Newcomb*, *Leutze* maneuvered clear to allow its crew to bring the flooding under control. Despite having its fantail almost severed, the destroyer was successfully towed to Kerama Retto for emergency repairs and then sent back to California, where it was declared a constructive total loss post-war. (NHHC)

The US Navy's entry into Lingayen Gulf prompted an intense Japanese reaction. Thirteen ships were hit on January 6, 1945, including the heavy cruiser USS *Louisville* (CA-28). As seen in these view, the suicide aircraft is just about to strike the cruiser. Fortunately for the ship's crew, the aircraft hit the heavily-armored face of 8in. Turret No. 2, which confined the damage to that area. Nevertheless, burning aviation fuel caused severe casualties totaling 36 dead and 56 wounded. (NARA)

Ultimately, suicide operations were unsustainable. It is important to note that even in April 1945, the heaviest month of kamikaze attacks, only 35 percent of Japanese sorties were conducted by kamikazes.

There were several major factors that limited the effectiveness of kamikaze attacks. A key issue was the poor or non-existent target recognition skills of the pilots conducting the attacks. This resulted in a severe problem with target selection. Simply put, the kamikazes were attacking too many destroyers and ignoring more lucrative targets such as loaded transports. The usual course of action for the inexperienced kamikaze pilot was to attack the first target that came into view. Too often, these were destroyers or smaller craft on picket duty. Between February and May 1945, 38 percent of kamikaze attacks were devoted to attacking destroyers and 45 percent to smaller ships and craft. This was a result of the Japanese strategy of reducing the radar picket line off Okinawa as a pre-requisite to attacking more lucrative targets. This strategy was unwise, since it focused on the type of target that was best able to defend itself by maneuver and firepower.

Another problem was the nature of the weapon itself. Although a kamikaze was a formidable vehicle of destruction, it typically possessed insufficient terminal velocity to penetrate deeply into a ship and cause mortal damage. In the great majority of cases in which a ship was mortally wounded by a kamikaze, the crippling damage was caused by the aircraft's bomb and not by the impact of the aircraft itself. This was particularly true with cruisers and battleships, which had armored decks. It is important to note that no cruiser or battleship was ever in danger of sinking as a result of kamikaze attack. A kamikaze could cause tremendous topside damage and often heavy personnel casualties from exposed antiaircraft gun crews, but it lacked the destructive power to sink large ships.

The exception to the rule that kamikazes were ineffective against large ships was their performance against aircraft carriers. These were unique targets, since they had ready sources of combustible items – fuel lines and aircraft loaded with fuel and ordnance – to start and sustain a conflagration. This danger was especially real in escort carriers, which lacked the firefighting capabilities and large damage-control crews embarked in fleet carriers. Arguably, carriers were the most important potential target for the kamikazes, and one against which they could be effective. The combustibility of carriers has already been mentioned, and added to this was the effect of explosions on the carriers' unarmored decks, which, even if they were not fatal, could force the ship out of action for an extended period.

In 1944, the kamikazes hit Essex-class fleet carriers six times, but none were placed in danger of sinking. A single Independence-class light carrier was also damaged. Escort carriers were more susceptible to kamikazes, with seven being damaged and one sunk by them. In 1945, the results were similar, with ten instances of fleet carriers being struck and none sunk, although one came close. Only a single light carrier was struck during this time and it survived. Escort carriers, however, were more often unable to control the large fires that could grow out of control after the initial hit. Nine were damaged in 1945 and two sunk. The US Navy was fortunate that the kamikazes did not focus their efforts on carriers. Ultimately, despite the kamikaze successes against carriers, it is important to note that the Fast Carrier Task Force was able to operate for more than 70 days within easy range of Japanese airfields on Kyushu and maintain sea and air control over Okinawa and surrounding waters.

Despite the statistics that highlight the damage caused by kamikazes, it is indisputable that the suicide attackers were unsuccessful in their desperate attempts to change the course of the war. As a military weapon, the kamikaze was ineffective in achieving its goals. The initial kamikaze attacks were insufficient to stop the American invasion of Leyte, and then even as the kamikaze program picked up speed, it was unable to stop or seriously hinder the invasion of Luzon. American losses were heavy, but were still at levels that could be sustained. Indeed, they were never close to impacting on future operations. Even at Okinawa, the efforts of the kamikazes were inadequate to even slow the pace of the American advance. The failure of the kamikaze as a military weapon was mirrored by its failure as a psychological weapon. The morale of the American sailor was unbroken by the onslaught. Short of surrender, the Japanese had no other option but to resort to suicide attacks. Even this desperate move was ultimately futile.

AFTERMATH

The ultimate test of the kamikaze never occurred. After Okinawa, the Japanese largely ceased kamikaze attacks. They wanted to preserve their remaining aircraft and fuel for the expected American attack on the home islands. The Americans did plan to invade – the landing on Kyushu was scheduled for November 1945, to be followed by a massive assault on the Tokyo-Yokohama area in March 1946. The landings would be preceded by intensive air operations to reduce the threat from Japanese conventional and suicide air attacks.

The Americans realized that the cessation of Japanese air operations after the Okinawa campaign was an attempt to build up strength to counter the invasion in November. They also correctly assessed that the Japanese reaction to the initial landings would be more intense than anything seen before. The intelligence assessment at the time called for kamikaze operations of 500–800 aircraft against the Kyushu invasion force before reverting to defensive operations in preparation for the main landing on Honshu.

The Americans did not foresee the scale of kamikaze operations planned by the Japanese. The actual number of aircraft available to the enemy at this time remains in question. The JAAF was "all-in" for kamikaze attacks in defense of the homeland. One source gives the August 1945 strength of the JAAF as 7,800 aircraft. Of these, 2,650 were allocated for kamikaze attacks (900 combat and 1,750 advanced trainer aircraft), 2,150 for conventional operations and 3,000 not immediately available (under repair or in storage). Once the aircraft intended as kamikazes were expended, the more experienced pilots – and their aircraft – used as escorts or for other conventional missions would be allocated for kamikaze missions. With this in mind, the majority of the JAAF would have been used for suicide attacks.

The IJNAF had been the original advocate of suicide attacks, and by August 1945 its preparations for a massive kamikaze assault were well advanced in terms of aircraft serviceability and dispersal. The three air fleets based in the homeland were allocated

5,350 aircraft, of which 3,675 were operational. This total did include large numbers of less-capable aircraft, including 223 floatplanes and 2,667 trainers. In addition, there were another 4,200 aircraft not ready or allocated to operational units.

The effectiveness of thousands of kamikaze attacks against the American invasion fleet is impossible to predict. Assuming the 5,350 aircraft designated for kamikazes attacks were employed as such, it is realistic to assume some 60 percent would get off the ground and conduct attacks. Based on the effectiveness rates from previous kamikaze efforts, this would equate to some 100 ships sunk, approximately 1,000 damaged and about 5,700 dead American sailors. This would have accounted for a significant proportion of the invasion fleet.

Such a linear approach to analyzing the effectiveness of kamikaze attacks in defense of Japan probably does not tell the entire story. The overwhelming Allied air superiority would have been focused on keeping kamikaze bases under constant attack, but even the most intense measures would not have succeeded in eliminating the kamikaze threat. In addition to having their bases under constant threat, kamikazes faced other difficulties such as inferior aircraft and inexperienced pilots, severe maintenance issues and command and control issues.

In spite of these difficulties, the Okinawa campaign provided a clear example of how massive waves of kamikazes and even on occasion small groups of suicide aircraft could penetrate the American fighter screen and reach attack positions. Once this occurred, no amount of antiaircraft fire could completely protect the fleet. However, just like off Okinawa, while the US Navy would have suffered losses in an invasion of Japan, the kamikazes almost certainly would not have been enough to stop or seriously disrupt the invasion. The goal of the kamikaze was to increase the toll of American lives. While this would have been achieved, it is impossible to predict whether it would have secured the overall Japanese goal of gaining some sort of negotiated peace.

How are kamikazes viewed today? In Japan, the fascination with the young men who volunteered to sacrifice themselves in defense of the homeland has increased following an immediate post-war period of abhorrence. The men who were sacrificed are remembered for their pure motives and held up by some as a model for the youth of today. Totally forgotten is the fact that their sacrifice was meaningless in a military sense. It accomplished nothing other than to increase the death and suffering on both sides. While it is true that the kamikaze was the only military option open to the Japanese by late 1944, it also demonstrated that the military position of Japan was hopeless and that the military leadership did not possess the moral courage to end the conflict, but instead hoped to prolong it using young kamikaze pilots.

A common scene at many Japanese airfields in the weeks after the war was the removal of propellers from any aircraft that might be used for unauthorized kamikaze missions after the ceasefire. This photograph was taken at the IJNAF's base at Atsugi, near Tokyo, and it features a variety of aircraft including "Frances" and "Judy" bombers. (NARA)

FURTHER READING

Becton, F. Julian, *The Ship That Would Not Die* (Prentice-Hall, Englewood Cliffs, New Jersey, 1980)

Campbell, John, *Naval Weapons of World War Two* (Naval Institute Press, Annapolis, Maryland, 2002)

Ewing, Steve, *Thach Weave* (Naval Institute Press, Annapolis, Maryland, 2004)

Frank, Richard B., *Downfall* (Random House, New York, 1999)

Friedman, Norman, *Naval Anti-aircraft Guns & Gunnery* (Naval Institute Press, Annapolis, Maryland, 2013)

Historical Section, G-2, GHQ, FEC, *Philippines Operations Record, Phase III Jan.– Aug. 1945* (Japanese Monograph 7)

Historical Section, G-2, GHQ, FEC, *Philippines Operations Record, Phase III Dec.– Aug. 1945* (Japanese Monograph 8)

Historical Section, G-2, GHQ, FEC, *4th Air Army Operations 1944–1945* (Japanese Monograph 12)

Historical Section, G-2, GHQ, FEC, *Air Operations on Iwo Jima and the Ryukyus* (Japanese Monograph 51)

Historical Section, G-2, GHQ, FEC, *Preparations for Operations in Defense of the Homeland, Jul. 1944–Jul. 1945* (Japanese Monograph 85)

Historical Section, G-2, GHQ, FEC, *Okinawa Operations Record* (Japanese Monograph 135)

Hoyt, Edwin P., *The Last Kamikaze* (Praeger, Westport, Connecticut, 1993)

Inoguchi, Rikihei and Nakajima, Tadashi, *The Divine Wind* (Naval Institute Press, Annapolis, Maryland, 1994)

Ishiguro, Ryusuke and Januszewski, Tadeusz, *Japanese Special Attack Aircraft and Flying Bombs* (Stratus, Sandomierz, Poland, 2009)

Millot, Bernard, *Divine Thunder* (McCall Publishing, New York, 1970)

Morison, Samuel Eliot, *Leyte, June 1944–January 1945* (Volume XII of History of United States Naval Operations in World War II) (Little Brown and Company, Boston, 1975)

Morison, Samuel Eliot, *The Liberation of the Philippines, Luzon, Mindanao, and the Visayas, 1944–1945* (Volume XIII of History of United States Naval Operations in World War II) (Little Brown and Company, Boston, 1975)

Morison, Samuel Eliot, *Victory in the Pacific 1945* (Volume XIV of History of United States Naval Operations in World War II) (Little Brown and Company, Boston, 1975)

Rielly, Robin L., *Kamikaze Attacks of World War II* (McFarland & Company, Jefferson, North Carolina, 2010)

Rielly, Robin L., *Kamikazes, Corsairs, and Picket Ships* (Casemate, Philadelphia, 2008)

Sears, David, *At War with the Wind* (Citadel Press, New York, 2008)

Sheftall, M. G., *Blossoms in the Wind* (New American Library, New York, 2006)

Smith, Peter C., *Kamikaze,* (Pen & Sword. Barnsley, South Yorkshire, 2014)

Stern, Robert C., *Fire from the Sky* (Naval Institute Press, Annapolis, Maryland, 2010)

Wallace, Robert E., *From Dam Neck to Okinawa* (Naval Historical Center, Washington, 2001)

Wukovits, John, *Hell from the Heavens* (Da Capo Press, Boston, 2015)

INDEX